8 Strategies for Engaging Boys in the Classroom

I0520956

A classroom guide for teachers
By Jeremy Spicer

Edited by Tonya Rozelle
Special thanks to Wendy Webb, Rebecca Thompson, and to the many others who contributed their input and editorial insight.

Cover photo by JustPhotof Photo & Video on Unsplash (used under Unsplash license).

Self Published by Jeremy Spicer
www.jeremyspicer.com

ISBN 979-8-9932617-0-6 (Paperback)

Other editions (forthcoming):
    Hardcover: 979-8-9932617-1-3
    eBook: 979-8-9932617-2-0
    Audiobook: 979-8-9932617-3-7
    (expected release February 2026)

First Edition
Printed in the United States of America.

Table of Contents

Introduction ii

Communication is Key...1

8 Strategies for Engaging Boys in the Classroom

#1 Be Active..13

Practical Strategies for Including More Active Learning

    A. Movement for Key Words...15

    B. Standing Up Whenever Possible 17

    C. Create Stations Around the Room 17

    D. Use Objects and Gadgets 18

    E. Unstructured Free Time..19

    F. Activity Sheets, Crafts, Games, and Puzzles 20

#2 Use Visuals 25

Practical Strategies for Using Visuals

    A. Images and Pictures 27

    B. Object Lessons...28

    C. Costumes and Props 29

#3 Allow for Competition...35

Practical Strategies for Incorporating Competition

    A. Games and Events..38

    B. Mix Up Teams 38

    C. Use Everyday Challenges...39

    D. Personal Challenges Within Academics 41

    E. Dealing With Loss and Failure..42

#4 Utilize Numbers and Facts 47

Practical Strategies for Incorporating Numbers and Facts

    A. Distances and Measurements..48

    B. Dates and Times 49

    C. Word Usage and Sentence Patterns 49

    D. Interesting Facts About People..50

    E. Special Events 50

Table of Contents

#5 Encourage Leadership and Responsibility 55

Practical Strategies for Developing Leadership Skills

    A. Time Management 58

    B. Classroom Responsibilities....................................59

    C. Teaching and Peer Support....................................60

    D. Ownership With Assignments 61

#6 Use Masculine Language 67

Practical Strategies for Including Masculine Language

    A. Speech and Tone..73

    B. A Space That Signals Strength and Purpose 75

    C. Incorporate Masculine Role Models 75

    D. Celebrate Strength Through Character.................76

#7 Permit Humor and Goofiness 81

Practical Strategies for Using Humor Effectively

    A. Model the Right Kind of Humor 86

    B. Set Clear Expectations 86

    C. Encourage and Reinforce Positive Humor............87

    D. Playful Exaggeration 88

    E. Lighthearted Goofiness..89

#8 Bring Back Rough Play 95

Practical Strategies for Including Rough Play

    A. Arm Wrestling..100

    B. Physical Responsibility Tasks...............................100

    C. Obstacle Courses...101

    D. Pushups, Jumping Jacks, and More....................102

    E. Running and Racing 103

    F. Punching Bags..104

    G. Playful Wrestling..104

    H. Let Them Climb 106

    I. Foam Swords and Toy Guns 107

Table of Contents

Dealing With Behavior Issues

Dealing With Behavior Issues...115

Respect as the Foundation...121

Dealing With Off-Task Behavior 133

7 Steps for Dealing With Off-Task Behavior
   1. Have Clear Expectations....................................135
   2. Practice Positive Reinforcement.........................136
   3. Utilize Physical Proximity...................................137
   4. Ask Questions 140
   5. Give Them Ownership 141
   6. Reset With Removal...142
   7. Implement Consequences 143

Standing Up to Deliberate Defiance...149
   1. Respond Immediately, No Debate 149
   2. Initiate an Appropriate Consequence..................150
   3. Ensure They Understand....................................151
   4. Focus on Positive Engagement...........................151
   5. Move On After Discipline 153

Coaching Boys Through Conflict With Each Other 159

Closing Thoughts..169

Recommended Reading 171

About the Author 173

Glossary of Key Terms 175

"How can the bird that is born for joy
Sit in a cage and sing?"

– The School Boy, by William Blake

Introduction

First, A Word of Encouragement

Before we begin, I want to express my heartfelt gratitude for all you do as a teacher. Teaching is more than a profession; it is a calling and a commitment to changing lives. Every day, you pour your time, energy, and wisdom into shaping minds and guiding hearts. Your work extends far beyond the classroom, and its impact is immeasurable. I deeply appreciate your dedication to this calling.

In the midst of everything you juggle—lesson planning, grading, meetings, trainings, and so much more—taking the time to understand and connect with boys is no small task. Teaching boys can be incredibly rewarding, but it also brings unique challenges. They often carry a lot of energy, curiosity, and unpredictability into the classroom. These qualities may stretch your patience and creativity, but they also create powerful opportunities for growth—for your students and for you.

If you have faced struggles in your teaching journey, do not be discouraged. Struggles are not a sign of failure; they are often the very path to growth. The fact that you are reading this book, seeking fresh insight, and working to improve, speaks volumes about the kind of teacher you are.

A Note for Female Educators

If you're a female teacher, this book will expand your already powerful toolkit. Your natural strengths—warmth, empathy, and relational connection—are essential to a healthy classroom. Nothing in this book seeks to diminish those qualities or suggest you need to become someone you're not. What you'll find here are complementary strategies that help you understand the masculine communication style—how boys naturally engage, and how they respond when teaching aligns with their design. Think of it like learning key phrases in a student's native language. You're not abandoning your own voice; you're adding new ways to reach students who think and communicate differently.

This book places strong emphasis on masculinity and masculine communication because that's the language boys speak. By blending your natural strengths with these insights, you'll create a more balanced classroom where all students thrive.

I encourage you to read with an open mind. Some of the ideas may feel unfamiliar or even challenge what you've always done. Teaching is about continually growing, learning, and adapting. Think of these strategies as enhancements, instead of corrections—practical additions to your already powerful skill set.

Along the way, I want you to feel encouraged, not criticized; supported, not scrutinized; inspired, not overwhelmed. What you bring to the classroom matters deeply, and your presence is vital and irreplaceable. At the same time, boys need a kind of communication that doesn't come naturally to most women and requires intentional effort. Ignoring that reality doesn't serve them—or you.

By combining your natural strengths with a deeper understanding of how boys engage the world around them, you can help them grow in ways they might not otherwise experience. That's not abandoning who you are—it's making who you are more effective for every student.

A Few Disclaimers...

Before we dive into the heart of this material, it will be helpful to start with a few disclaimers.

1. Yes, These Are Generalizations

Much of what you'll read in this book involves broad generalizations about boys and girls. While these general statements can be helpful, they may not necessarily apply to every individual the same. Everyone is unique, shaped by personality, upbringing, and lived experience. So while many boys and girls exhibit the traits discussed within these pages, there will always be exceptions. Consider these insights as a general guide, not a strict rule.

2. Most of These Strategies Will Work for Girls Too

Although this book focuses on boys, many of these strategies will benefit girls as well. Think of it like clothing —boys' clothes often work fine for girls, but not always the other way around. Similarly, teaching methods that work well for boys often benefit girls, but strategies designed specifically for girls don't always work with boys.

3. Nothing Works 100% of the Time

Even the best implementation of these strategies will fall flat now and then. Kids are human, and so are you. Some days they're tired or overwhelmed. Some days you are, too. Progress might feel slow, and success might not always look the way you hoped. That doesn't mean you're doing anything wrong. It just means that sometimes, no matter how hard you try, it's not going to work. This is part of the messy, beautiful process we call teaching. Not everything in this book will work for your situation, and that's okay.

4. Use Caution for Special Education and Learners with Diverse Learning Needs

This book is primarily written with standard classroom environments in mind. Many of the strategies shared can be helpful for Special Education and students who have diverse learning needs, but they may not apply as effectively in every situation. These students face unique challenges, and what works for one may not work for another. While it's worth trying these ideas when appropriate, they should be applied thoughtfully and with flexibility. Always prioritize the guidance of parents, the direction provided in IEPs, and your own knowledge of individual students.

The Goal of This Book

The goal of this book is simple: to equip you with tools and insights that will help you understand the language of boys. I want to help you create a classroom where boys feel understood, engaged, and motivated to learn—not one where they feel constantly corrected, misunderstood, or shut down. Teaching boys can be effective and not just about managing behavior or delivering content; it's about building a space where they can thrive. It means adding a few more tools to your toolbox—strategies that meet boys where they are and fit who they are.

How To Use This Book

You are most likely already using a few of these strategies, and that's great! Take this opportunity to revisit some with fresh eyes, or explore ways to expand on what you're already doing. Sometimes, even familiar strategies can gain new life with a slight shift in approach.

There is no required order to these eight strategies. Feel free to jump in wherever it seems most helpful for your setting or situation. Each strategy stands on its own, so you can start with the one that speaks to your current needs or challenges.

Don't feel pressured to apply everything all at once. Instead, pick one strategy to focus on. Give yourself time, tweak it, and let it become part of your natural rhythm. Once you've gotten comfortable with one, come back and explore another. It's always better to try new things slowly —discover what works and what doesn't, and make any needed adjustments for your situation. Each class is different. What worked one year may not the next. The same is true in reverse: what didn't work one year may work the next.

This is a book you can revisit again and again. Over time, rereading certain sections can reinforce key practices or spark new ideas you might have missed before. As your experience grows, so will your insight into how these strategies can support the boys you teach.

Above all, I hope this book feels like a helpful, encouraging companion as you continue the important work of teaching boys well. I'm excited for you!

Sources and Supportive Research

This book is not to serve as a research paper or an academic analysis of the topics discussed. My focus is on practical application—what to do and how to do it. Rather than presenting extensive academic research throughout the text, my goal is to synthesize multiple insights into a cohesive plan of action that teachers can immediately apply.

For that reason, this book will not focus on citing sources in the traditional academic sense. However, I have included a list of recommended reading at the back of the book for those who wish to explore the research behind these ideas more deeply.

While much of the content is drawn from my personal experience, observations, and conversations with active educators, the concepts presented are not merely opinions. They align with established research and are supported by years of studies in education, child development, and gendered learning. Readers can verify and expand on these ideas through the recommended resources or by exploring additional research independently, which I encourage.

Final Preface

Teaching boys can be one of the most rewarding—and sometimes most challenging—experiences in a classroom.

Over the years, I've watched countless boys light up when a lesson connects, and I've seen the same boys disconnect or act out when the approach doesn't match the way they naturally engage with the world around them.

This book is written for teachers who want to understand boys on a deeper level, not just manage behavior and deliver content. It's about seeing boys as they are, recognizing their strengths, and providing an environment where they can thrive academically, socially, and emotionally.

Before diving into the eight strategies, it's important to step back and consider the foundation of all effective teaching: communication. Understanding how boys and girls naturally engage with the world—and how your classroom communicates—will set the stage for everything that follows.

Let's begin by exploring the essential principles of classroom communication and how they can transform your classroom, laying the foundation for the eight strategies—followed by guidance on addressing behavior issues.

Communication is Key

It Starts With Communication

It's often said that most problems in life stem from communication errors. How much more when it comes to teaching? At its core, teaching is more than just delivering information; it's about effective communication and connection. Your students need to understand your message in a way that resonates with their learning style. If the right connection isn't established, your message will never reach them.

Without effective communication, you risk losing students' attention and creating frustration for both them and yourself. We've all been there: we carefully craft a lesson, give clear instructions, yet somehow there are always students who seem disengaged. They fidget, lose focus, test boundaries, and before long, you find yourself managing behavior more than teaching.

The way we communicate as teachers has a profound impact on a student's learning experience. If the classroom communication style doesn't align with how a student naturally processes and responds to information, that student may quickly become disconnected, disengaged, discouraged, or even disruptive (the four D's, as I like to say).

It's no secret that boys and girls communicate differently. Spend a few minutes observing people at work or play, and you'll notice distinct differences in how they interact. These differences reflect not just personality but fundamental ways in which boys and girls naturally engage with each other and the world around them. Before diving into strategies for reaching boys, it's essential to understand and explore these differences further.

The Different World of Girls and Boys

From an early age, girls tend to develop strong verbal skills and use language as their primary means of communication. They engage in face-to-face, eye-to-eye conversations, speak in complete thoughts, ask detailed questions, outwardly express emotions, and build relationships. Social connection is central to their interactions, and much of their play revolves around cooperative activities where communication, connection, and relationships are key.

Girls also gravitate toward environments that feel safe, structured, orderly, and visually appealing. They are drawn to spaces that provide comfort and security: rooms decorated with colors, soft cushions, pleasant aromas, sparkly or cute items, and neatly arranged materials. These elements help foster connection and promote emotional safety, reinforcing their preferred way of engaging with the world.

Boys, on the other hand, are wired for action and tend to communicate physically first and verbally second. While they are capable of verbal expression, their natural inclination is to engage with the world through movement, activity, and direct interaction. Instead of talking through emotions or social situations, boys often express themselves through touching—rough play, competition, or physical challenges. Watch a group of boys during free time, or recess, and you'll see energy in motion: running, climbing, jumping, wrestling, and competing in games involving chasing, tagging, or mock battles.

Boys' social connections are built more through shared activities than extended conversations. Loud voices, playful jabs, and bursts of movement are all forms of communication, ways of establishing camaraderie and testing the boundaries. In contrast to girls, boys' communication tends to be more aggressive, action-driven, and rooted in movement.

Boys also often focus on logical processes and internal problem-solving rather than verbalizing thoughts and feelings. Many boys think silently, processing information internally before speaking, if they choose to speak at all. This difference becomes especially striking in adolescence. A group of teenage boys can sit together, bond, and share companionship without saying a word. Their connection with each other depends on shared experience rather than continuous conversation.

These differences reflect fundamental distinctions in communication styles that profoundly impact learning and classroom interaction. And this is just a small glimpse of the vast differences between boys and girls. Understanding these distinctions is crucial when designing classroom environments that meet the needs of all students.

The Silent Language of the Classroom

Communication isn't only about the words we speak; it extends to the environment we create. Classroom communication encompasses the entire setting—from the physical layout of a room to unspoken rules that shape daily interactions.

Every detail in your classroom sends a message. The colors and posters around the room, the arrangement and type of furniture, body language, and even the behaviors that are encouraged or discouraged all contribute to the language of the space. Before a single word is spoken, the environment of a room is already communicating. Key elements include:

- Classroom Layout
- Color Schemes/Posters
- Type of Furniture
- Teacher's Body Language
- Classroom Culture/Atmosphere
- Verbal and Nonverbal Cues

A lesson can be well-structured, but if the environment doesn't foster engagement or support the message, even the best content will struggle to make an impact. Take a step back and evaluate your classroom through a fresh lens. Every element, both spoken and unspoken, shapes how students feel, behave, and learn. When teachers view their classroom as a complete communication system rather than just a space where lessons are delivered, they unlock a powerful tool for keeping students motivated and engaged.

The Voice of the Classroom

Have you considered the voice and communication style of your classroom—whether it leans more feminine or masculine? Many teachers don't. Why would they? As educators, we are trained to follow a certain approach, and few of us stop to question it. Take a moment and think about your classroom based on what you've been reading in this chapter. Does it align more with how girls process information or boys?

Most classrooms naturally align with how girls process information. Why? In part, because the majority of teachers—especially in preschool and elementary—are female. Teachers shape learning environments based on what feels natural and effective to them, so it makes sense that classrooms often reflect the communication styles and preferences female educators find most intuitive. Like anyone else, a female teacher will naturally create a space where she feels comfortable, connected, and where her methods resonate with her instincts.

Over time, as women have continued to make up the vast majority of the teaching profession, classroom environments have gradually taken on a communication style that aligns more closely with how girls engage with the world—not boys.

Let's take décor as an example. Imagine women designing a room for themselves. What colors, furniture, and decorations would they choose? Now imagine men doing the same for themselves. What would a masculine room look like as compared to a feminine one? How different would the colors, textures, and objects be? Now, imagine designing a room for children. What colors, textures, and objects would it include? Compared to the masculine and feminine rooms, the child's room would almost certainly resemble the feminine one more closely. Why? Because environments for children are largely shaped and influenced by women, reflecting a more feminine voice.

The example above is more obvious with younger students, but the underlying principles carry into the older grades, because the influence extends far beyond physical classroom design. It shapes every aspect of school life—behavior expectations, lesson planning, instructional methods, classroom layout, recess structures, and more.

It doesn't stop at the classroom level. This influence extends across the entire educational system. Schools throughout America largely reflect a female-centered model, favoring traits and behaviors commonly associated with how girls learn—sitting still, working quietly, and completing structured tasks. Boys, who tend to be more active, physical, and competitive, often struggle to adapt because the dominant communication style leans far more feminine than masculine.

One simple example is how teachers plan class groupings and grade levels each year. Teachers often focus on relational factors—who gets along, preventing social conflict, and ensuring no one feels isolated. This reflects a more feminine approach that values social harmony, emotional safety, and personal connection. Male educators may approach it differently, emphasizing balanced strengths, fostering competition, or even assigning classes at random to build adaptability.

This contrast illustrates a broader difference in teaching styles. Neither approach is inherently right or wrong; rather, it shows how the feminine voice has come to dominate and become the gold standard for the education system.

The reality is that when any group shapes an environment, it reflects that group's strengths, preferences, and communication style. Recognizing this dominant influence helps explain why many boys struggle to thrive in traditional classrooms.

Think about your own students for a moment: Who do you struggle with most? Who has the hardest time following instructions? Who tends to be at the center of behavior issues? Who is most often medicated for focus issues? More often than not, the answer is boys.

The problem isn't that boys are more difficult or inattentive. The problem is that they're being asked to function in an environment that doesn't share their natural communication style, albeit unintentionally.

Imagine being placed in a room where instructions are given in a language you barely understand—where expectations are built around a way of thinking that feels foreign. How long would you stay engaged before you began to check out or act out?

That's exactly what many boys experience every day. It's not that they don't want to learn—it's that the way they learn is often misunderstood, overlooked, or even shamed in the classroom. But when teachers adjust their approach to better match how boys communicate and engage, everything changes. Behavior improves. Focus increases. And learning comes alive.

The Consequences of Mismatched Communication

For decades, behaviors once considered normal for boys—restlessness, rough play, challenging authority, and a constant need for movement—have increasingly been labeled as disruptive, inappropriate, or problematic. Traits that were once understood as part of healthy boyhood are now too often viewed through the lens of disorder or defiance. What used to be dismissed as "boys being boys" is now frequently interpreted as a behavioral issue that needs correction or control.

Psychologist Michael Thompson, co-author of *Raising Cain: Protecting the Emotional Life of Boys*, observes that in many classrooms, behavioral standards reflect what comes more naturally to girls, while boys are often treated as "defective girls." In other words, when boys do not conform to a more verbal, still, and emotionally expressive model of learning, they are seen as broken rather than different.

The truth is that many boys who act out are not misbehaving—they are communicating. Their restlessness, noise, and constant movement are their native language. Boys tend to process emotion, stress, and learning through action, not through long periods of quiet reflection or verbal discussion. Yet in many classrooms, this "language of movement" is silenced. They are told, directly or indirectly, that their way of engaging and learning is unacceptable.

When a boy continually receives this message, one of two instinctive responses usually emerges:

- **The Fight Response**: Boys who respond with defiance challenge authority, talk back, or push against rules. They may act out physically, pick fights, or become the class "troublemaker." These boys aren't angry by nature—they're frustrated. When they feel misunderstood or out of place, aggression becomes their way of regaining control and significance.

- **The Flight Response**: These boys withdraw, stop trying, stop participating, and retreat into silence or apathy. They may appear unmotivated or disinterested, but underneath they feel discouraged, disconnected, and defeated. Believing their natural

impulses are unwelcome, they shut down
emotionally and academically.

If this sounds familiar, you're likely seeing the classic
"fight or flight" response in action. It's not rebellion or
laziness—it's survival. When boys feel they cannot succeed
or be accepted within the classroom's dominant style of
communication, their psyche shifts into protection mode.

And the outcome is costly. Boys stop thriving.
Teachers become frustrated. Parents grow defensive.
Classrooms turn into battlegrounds rather than places of
growth. Everyone loses.

But this pattern is not inevitable. When teachers
recognize that boys' behavior is often a form of
communication rather than defiance, loss of engagement
rather than laziness, they can begin to respond differently
—by meeting boys where they are, helping them translate
their energy into engagement, and restoring a sense of
belonging to the learning environment.

The Key to Reaching Boys

So, what's the solution? The goal isn't to suppress boys
or reshape them to fit the current classroom model—it's to
reshape the model itself so that it works for all students,
including boys. Boys don't need to be fixed; the system
does. We must move from trying to make boys more
compliant to helping them become more connected.

This doesn't mean catering exclusively to boys or
creating an environment that leaves girls behind. It means
designing classrooms that value and engage both. Boys and
girls are not opposites—they are complementary learners.
They process information differently, respond to different
kinds of motivation, and communicate in distinct ways.
When we honor those differences instead of trying to erase
them, everyone benefits.

As teachers, our task is to work with a boy's natural
design, not against it. That means channeling his energy

rather than punishing it, using movement to unlock focus, and viewing competition and physicality not as problems or distractions, but as pathways to learning. It means recognizing that boys often express emotion through action rather than words, and that their desire to test limits is often a search for respect and relationship, not rebellion.

As a male teacher, I share this communication style. I understand the unspoken language of boys—the way they use humor to connect, movement to think, and rough play to bond. I've seen how a simple shift in approach can completely change a boy's attitude toward learning. When you engage a boy through his natural instincts—through visuals, action, structure, and purpose—he doesn't just pay attention; he comes alive.

When teachers communicate in a way that makes sense to boys—using masculine language—everything changes. Learning becomes exciting instead of exhausting. Behavior issues become opportunities for growth rather than daily battles. Boys who once seemed unreachable begin to participate, contribute, and lead. And perhaps most importantly, they have a place to belong.

By using strategies that align with how boys naturally process information, you will not only enhance their learning experience but also rediscover the joy and effectiveness in your own teaching. A classroom that works for boys works better for everyone—it's more dynamic, engaging, and balanced.

In the chapters ahead, you'll discover eight strategies designed to help you connect with boys and unlock their full potential. These are not just behavior management tools or motivational tricks—they are frameworks for transformation. They will help you build trust, spark curiosity, ignite a love for learning, and shape boys into confident, capable young men.

When you begin to speak the masculine language, you'll see walls come down, confidence rise, and behavior improve. Students who once seemed distant or defiant will begin to engage, not because they have changed, but because the classroom has.

Are you ready to take your classroom to the next level —to inspire, to lead, and to make a lasting impact? Then let's begin.

8 Strategies for Engaging Boys in the Classroom

"Movement, or physical activity, is thus an essential factor in intellectual growth."

— Maria Montessori

#1 Be Active

Boys Learn Best When They Move

Let's start with the obvious: boys are active! If you've spent any amount of time around boys, you know this one well. It's not just a personality trait—it's core to who they are. Movement is essential to how boys experience and engage the world around them. Boys need to move, and they learn best when they are physically active. Unfortunately, the gold standard in many classrooms—sitting still, staying quiet, and keeping hands to oneself—is the exact opposite of what boys need in order to thrive academically.

That's not to say boys shouldn't learn the discipline of sitting still and keeping their hands to themselves. These are essential life skills, and yes, boys should be guided in developing them. There is a time and place for sitting quietly and focusing on self-control. But this discussion is not about those moments—this is about what boys need most of the time in order to learn effectively.

The reality is, boys are more productive, more attentive, and more successful learners when they are allowed to move. The more movement that is incorporated into learning, the more likely boys are to stay engaged and actually retain what they're being taught. Movement helps regulate their energy, sharpen focus, and reinforce memory. Simply put, motion fuels cognition.

As a teacher, your goal should be to transform as many parts of your lesson as possible into active learning experiences. This doesn't mean letting them go crazy, it means deliberately planning activities that channel boys' energy into meaningful learning. Let them move between stations, build models, act out a scene, toss a ball while answering review questions, or use tools and materials to explore a concept with their hands. Learning becomes more effective when their bodies are involved.

It's important to be clear: conversation and small-group discussions, though useful in other ways, do not count as active learning for boys. Some educators assume that open discussion is a form of engagement, and while it may benefit verbal learners or provide social interaction, it does not meet the physical learning needs of most boys. Talking is still sitting, and sitting is still passive.

When talking about active learning for boys, I mean literal, physical movement. I'll never forget one fourth grader who was telling me about a project he was working on while simultaneously throwing kicks in the air. The topic had nothing to do with the topic of kicking, but the movement was part of how he focused and expressed himself while talking to me.

The bottom line is simple: boys need to move. Their bodies are wired for activity, and their brains process information more effectively when that energy has an outlet. Instead of fighting against this reality or demanding complete stillness, teachers can lean into it. Movement doesn't have to be a distraction—it can be a tool. When we harness boys' natural drive to move, we don't just keep them engaged—we open the door for deeper learning, stronger memory, and greater participation.

Practical Strategies for Including More Active Learning

There are many creative ways to add movement to the classroom. Teachers have developed various techniques over the years. I'm sure you are using many of these already. I encourage you to continue to explore and find new ways to keep boys active while learning.

A. Movement for Key Words

Incorporating a type of movement into your teaching when using key words is an excellent way to keep students engaged while reinforcing key concepts. Whether working with small children or teenagers, adding physical actions to certain words can boost attention and improve retention.

Younger Students

Younger students love to put their whole bodies into their movements. They thrive on active participation. When you say a certain word, students can:

- Clap their hands
- Stomp their feet
- Wiggle their bodies
- Wave their arms
- Tap their desks
- Change seats
- Flap arms for birds
- Climbing motion for trees

 Tips:

1. Keep keyword-actions manageable; too many words can become confusing.

2. Use words that appear frequently in the lesson. Words only mentioned a few times won't hold their interest.

3. Incorporate props like small hand-held objects, like a pencil, that can be shaken, tapped, or raised at the right moment.

Older Students

Older students may not respond to the same level of physical engagement as younger children, but movement-based learning can still be effective when adapted appropriately. Instead of the motions already mentioned, try these approaches:

- Standing for Key Terms: Have students stand up or switch seats whenever a keyword is mentioned. This works especially well in review sessions or vocabulary drills.

- Interactive Note-Taking: Instead of passive listening, encourage students to highlight, underline, or jot down a symbol when they hear key phrases. Be sure to pause and give time for marking.

- Classroom Walk & Talk: Have students walk slowly around the room with you as you teach.

- Hand Signals & Gestures: Rather than using large body movements, teens can use thumbs up/down, finger snaps, or subtle hand gestures to signal understanding or engagement with a concept.

- Competitive Elements: Turn key terms into a quick-response game where the first person to recognize and act on the word earns a small point or privilege.

 Tips:

1. Teens enjoy childish things but don't want to be treated like children. Strive to balance embracing their childlike impulses without being overly childish.

2. Involve them in the process of creating the movement— Their creativity may surprise you.

3. Keep it fresh. While consistency is helpful for both teachers and students, it's important to change things up occasionally rather than repeating the same motions every time.

Regardless of the age group, integrating movement when using certain words into lessons helps to ensure students are actively engaged rather than passively absorbing information. Adjusting techniques to fit different developmental levels makes learning more memorable and effective for all.

B. Standing Up Whenever Possible

Something as simple as standing up can make a big difference in attention for boys. Try incorporating standing up randomly during lessons—have students stand up and sit down a few times just for fun, turning it into a silly game.

For example, I'll suddenly pause teaching and ask everyone to stand, then sit, then repeat a few times. Once they catch on, the giggles begin—younger kids love this!

Standing also works well during memorizing or call-and-response phrases. You can have them walk around the room or play a quick game of "follow the leader." Even small tasks—like grabbing supplies or flipping on a light switch—can help boys reset their focus, just by getting them out of their seats.

Tips:

1. Give permission to stand at their desk while instruction is happening as long as it's not distracting.

2. Set clear expectations for when standing is allowed and when it's not.

3. Avoid too much standing and moving around as this can get out of hand very quickly.

C. Create Stations Around the Room

Divide your lesson into separate stations around the room and have the students move from station to station with you while teaching. This method works well for smaller groups. Hands-on activities at each station can enhance engagement even more.

For larger groups that are too difficult to move, you should become the moving target. Create different points in the room where you, rather than the students, move to while teaching. Moving across the room in different patterns forces students to move their heads and bodies to keep up with you. Even shifting to the other side of the room while teaching can help reset attention. The more space you use, the better.

Whichever method you choose, try to keep things moving. Avoid staying at a single station for too long. If you're the one moving, consider shifting at least every major point or every 30-60 seconds. If students are moving, try to keep each station under 5–10 minutes, depending on the age and activity.

Tips:

1. Too many stations can be complicated to manage; keep it simple.

2. Depending on the situation, you can make stations voluntary, giving them the option to focus on the one they prefer.

D. Use Objects and Gadgets

Objects that can be touched or held significantly enhance learning and retention—especially if they can be taken apart! Boys love knowing how things work, and taking things apart is always a big win.

Of course, allowing students to handle objects will come with a few challenges of its own. Items may get messy, used in unintended ways, even broken or lost. This is normal and part of the process. Just plan for it.

If using an object gets messy, have students help clean up afterward and build in extra time. If you're worried about an object breaking, bring extras or use a replica. If you have only one item, give each student a few seconds to hold it before passing it around. If an object is too valuable or fragile, show it to them and then have them create their own version through drawing or craft materials while you talk about it.

The more your lessons incorporate tangible objects that can be actively used, the more students will remember the material.

Tips:

1. Use the classic show and tell method, having students bring or create their own items that relate to the lesson.

2. Having too many objects is like having too many main points. Keep it simple and stick with only a few objects, depending on the lesson.

E. Unstructured Free Time

Although the above strategies are designed to incorporate movement during instruction, sometimes boys simply need unstructured time to "get the wiggles out." Even a brief break—just one to three minutes—can make a noticeable difference. Many teachers refer to this as a "Brain Break."

If you're worried about things getting too rowdy, offer a few specific active options. By giving structured choices, you maintain control while still allowing the freedom boys need to move and reset.

Tips:

1. The most you will need for this is 3-5 minutes.

2. This is best done independently, not as a social time like recess.

F. Activity Sheets, Crafts, Games, and Puzzles

Activity pages, crafts, and games are great tools for keeping things active and engaging. These don't necessarily have to relate directly to the lesson, but making a connection can reinforce learning.

If you don't have an activity sheet, give students a blank piece of paper and ask them to draw or write something related to the lesson. Older students can create their own game that parallels the lesson. Be creative and make it fun!

Tips:

1. Keep a few extra ideas ready to go just in case.

2. Fidget toys, such as Rubik's Cubes, are good ways to keep boys moving without too much disturbance. And yes, most boys are really listening, even when it seems they aren't.

In Summary

Movement isn't optional for boys—it's essential. By making active learning your default approach, you transform classroom management from constant redirection to natural engagement. Boys who once seemed restless become focused. Those who appeared defiant become invested. Classrooms that rely solely on passive learning risk disengaging boys, limiting their ability to absorb and apply new knowledge.

Incorporating movement—through hands-on projects, interactive lessons, or even short physical breaks—does more than burn off energy. It improves focus, retention, and engagement, creating a dynamic learning environment where boys can participate fully. When teachers recognize that boys learn best by doing, they can design lessons that align with their strengths, spark curiosity, and invite problem-solving in ways that feel natural and meaningful.

Spend time observing boys at play and you'll see how instinctively they engage the world through action—running, climbing, building, kicking, wrestling, and exploring with their bodies. This physical exploration is not random; it is how they process information, test ideas, and make sense of their surroundings. By embracing this active learning style, teachers connect with how boys think, communicate, and learn, creating a classroom environment that values movement as a tool for understanding rather than a distraction.

Ultimately, active teaching isn't just a strategy—it's a philosophy. It recognizes and honors the natural energy, curiosity, and physical intelligence of boys. When lessons are designed to move, create, and engage, boys feel seen, understood, and capable of learning at their best. Active classrooms are not only more engaging—they cultivate confidence, problem-solving skills, and a love of learning that carries beyond the school day. For boys, learning through movement isn't an exception to the rule—it's the key to unlocking their potential.

Reflection Questions

1. How often do I currently incorporate movement into my lessons with boys? Should I include more?

2. Do I view physical activity as a distraction or as a valuable part of learning? Why?

3. What differences have I noticed in boys' engagement or behavior when they are allowed to move versus when they are expected to sit still?

4. What messages might I unintentionally be sending about movement and energy in the classroom or group setting?

5. Have I created an environment that values boys' natural need for activity, or one that suppresses it?

Application Questions

1. What is one way I can intentionally build movement into my next lesson or group activity?

2. How can I provide short, structured breaks or physical transitions to help boys reset and stay focused?

3. What routines or systems could I establish that allow boys to move with purpose (e.g., classroom jobs, active learning stations)?

4. What outdoor or physically engaging activities can I plan this week to reinforce a key concept in my lesson?

5. How can I reframe moments of restlessness as opportunities to connect with how boys learn best?

"A picture is worth a thousand words."
– Frederick R. Barnard

#2 Use Visuals

Boys Are Visually Stimulated Learners

Boys are naturally wired for visual stimulation. Have you ever noticed how quickly boys get distracted by movement? Whether it's the flickering flame of a fire, a bird flying past the window, or a ball bouncing down the hallway, boys are drawn to things they can see and track. Their eyes are always scanning, locking in on motion, light, shape, and space. This isn't a fault or a sign of inattentiveness—it's part of how they're designed to explore and engage with the world. Boys are often visual explorers long before they become verbal processors. Visual cues are central to how they interpret, understand, and remember information.

You've probably heard the Fredrick Barnard quote before, "A picture is worth a thousand words." When it comes to teaching boys, this couldn't be more true. A well-placed visual often conveys meaning more effectively than a lengthy explanation. Rather than talking circles around a concept, try showing them what you mean. A simple diagram, object, or action can go further than words and explanations. Boys tend to remember what they see long after they've forgotten what they heard. Visuals create mental hooks—just look at the power of social media. We can use the same principle to anchor learning in the classroom.

When planning lessons, think "Show and Tell"—but lean heavily on the show. Reinforcing verbal instruction with visual aids boosts attention, improves understanding, and makes the learning stick. This could be as simple as writing a key word on the board in bold colors, using hand gestures while you explain a new idea, or physically acting out a process. If you're teaching about character development, don't just describe it—use story illustrations, draw it out, or assign roles and have students act out a scene.

Even better, involve the boys in creating the visuals. Let them draw the story as you tell it. Invite them to build a model of what you're describing using blocks, clay, or classroom materials. Challenge them to sketch a diagram on the board or illustrate a key idea. This taps into their creativity, makes the lesson more interactive, and reinforces the content through action.

As an added bonus, visuals help teachers too. Many educators find that using images, props, or object lessons keeps them on track, reducing the temptation to over-explain or wander off-topic. Let's be honest—we've all taken a lesson down a few unnecessary rabbit trails. A strong visual cue brings clarity and helps make abstract or complex ideas more concrete. It acts as a silent partner in your teaching, guiding both you and your students through the material.

And remember—visuals don't have to be complicated. Sometimes all it takes is holding up a common object or displaying a single image. A jar of sand, a flashlight, a rope —everyday items can become powerful teaching tools when paired with the right story or explanation. For younger students—especially preschoolers—a "mystery box" filled with lesson-related items revealed one at a time can create a sense of wonder and anticipation. The suspense alone can hold their attention far longer than any speech ever could.

In short, visuals aren't just helpful—they're essential. They speak the language of boys. If you want your message to stick, don't just say it—show it.

Practical Strategies for Using Visuals

Collaborate with fellow teachers and explore visual strategies that suit your students and your teaching style. There are countless great ideas out there; here are a few that have proven effective over the years. Use them individually or combine them—but don't overload your lesson. A balanced approach will keep students engaged without overwhelming them with too many visuals.

A. Images and Pictures

Why spend five minutes explaining something when one picture can communicate it instantly? Visuals grab attention, clarify meaning, and add those thousand words to your lesson.

That said, avoid the dreaded "Death by PowerPoint" approach. Instead of cluttered slides and clip art, use real-life images, short videos, animations, or even memes and GIFs when appropriate. Keep it relevant, simple, and clear.

Pictures are especially powerful when telling stories or explaining history and science. For example, if you're talking about a historical event, show photos of the people involved, locations, or artifacts from that time period. Don't limit yourself to just two or three images—swap visuals often to maintain interest and pace.

 Tips:

1. Avoid visuals that are too busy or overloaded with information.

2. Use visuals to reinforce key points, not minor details.

3. Preview every image and video beforehand. Look closely for background elements that might be distracting or inappropriate for your age group.

B. Object Lessons

Object lessons are one of the most powerful ways to visually demonstrate abstract concepts (my go-to strategy). By taking something familiar and using it to illustrate a much deeper meaning, you create an unforgettable experience for students of any age.

If you're unsure how to create an object lesson, there are plenty of ideas available online. Simply search for your lesson topic or key word along with "object lesson," and you'll find numerous creative examples. Of course, you can also craft your own by breaking down the key concept and finding a physical representation—something your audience is already familiar with.

For example, let's say you're teaching the importance of applying knowledge rather than just learning it. A glass of milk and chocolate syrup will easily and visually help illustrate this.

Pour the syrup into the milk, but don't stir it up. Take a sip and say, "This doesn't taste like chocolate milk, but I added chocolate! What's wrong?" Without fail, the students will tell you that you need to stir it up. This is your teaching moment! Explain that just adding chocolate isn't enough to make chocolate milk; we must mix it up! In the same way, just as mixing the syrup is necessary to make chocolate milk, knowing something isn't enough—we must put it into action.

This kind of visual demonstration ensures the lesson sticks far better than words alone.

Tips:

1. Rehearse more complex object lessons beforehand and have extra supplies nearby in case anything goes wrong.

2. When possible, involve students directly. Participation makes the experience more memorable.

3. Let the object do the talking. Use clear, concise language and avoid over-explaining. Keep the focus on the visual aid.

C. Costumes and Props

Simple props and costume accessories can bring lessons to life in a vivid and engaging way. You don't need a full costume or theatrical performance to make an impact —even something as small as a pencil or plant can add a visual element that reinforces your teaching and keeps students focused.

For example, if you're telling a story with three characters and it's just you, assign each character a simple prop like a hat, scarf, or pair of glasses. Switch props as you switch roles so students can easily follow who's speaking. No props? Use distinct gestures, voice changes, or different positions in the room to help students track the characters.

Props aren't just for storytelling. A magnifying glass can turn a lesson into a detective mission. A chef's hat can introduce a "recipe" for solving a math problem. Sunglasses might signal a laid-back review session. These small additions spark imagination and set a playful, engaging tone.

Bright clothing and novelty accessories—like bold colors or oversized items—naturally grab attention and help capture boys' focus. Boys instinctively track movement, so using your hands to hold or move an object draws their eyes in and keeps them engaged. These simple strategies use visual and physical cues to make your teaching more dynamic and memorable.

Tips:

1. Don't overdo it—too many props can become distracting, for both you and the students (unless that is the point you are trying to make).

2. Use items that are easy to put on and remove (like jackets, scarves, or glasses). Avoid anything that requires pulling over the head or getting stuck.

In Summary

Boys are naturally drawn to movement and visual stimulation—far more than to lengthy verbal instruction. It's not that they can't listen or won't pay attention; it's that their brains are built to respond first to what they see. Understanding this fundamental truth can completely transform how you teach. Once you begin aligning your methods with the way boys are wired to learn, everything starts to shift—attention improves, engagement increases, and learning deepens.

That's why visual tools like images, object lessons, props, and demonstrations aren't just extras—they're essential. These tools tap into a boy's natural learning style, turning passive listening into active participation. Whether it's a chart that maps out a process, a dramatic object lesson that illustrates a truth, or simply holding up a physical item that connects to the day's theme, visuals give boys something to hook onto—a concrete point of reference that anchors the abstract.

And here's the good news: you don't need to overhaul your whole curriculum. Small adjustments in how you present material can make a huge difference. A picture on the board, a labeled diagram, or a quick sketch can refocus wandering eyes. Breaking up a lesson with a physical demonstration or hands-on illustration can reignite interest and draw boys back into the content.

When boys are visually engaged, they stay focused longer, absorb more information, and—perhaps most importantly—begin to enjoy the learning process. Lessons that once felt like a chore become something to look forward to. The more interactive, hands-on, and visually stimulating your lessons are, the more likely your message will stick long-term. And when boys walk away not only having heard the truth but having seen and experienced it, that's a win for everyone.

Reflection Questions

1. When you think back to your own learning experiences, how did visuals help (or not help) you understand new ideas?

2. Have you noticed how boys in your group respond differently to visual input compared to verbal instruction?

3. Are there times when your teaching relies too heavily on words? What might you change for visual learners?

4. Do you find it easier or harder to stay focused when using visuals in your own teaching? Why do you think that is?

5. What keeps you from using more visual tools in your lessons—time, resources, confidence, or something else?

Application Questions

1. Choose one upcoming lesson and identify a simple visual element you could add (an image, object, prop, or video).

2. Create or adapt an object lesson to help boys grasp a big idea you're teaching this month.

3. Look through your teaching supplies—what props or costume pieces could you start using to bring your lessons to life?

4. Plan one short story or explanation where you swap out most of the words for images or actions. Try it and observe the results.

5. Make a checklist of three visual strategies you can commit to using in the next three weeks (like images, props, or demonstrations).

"The best competition I have is against myself to become better." – John Wooden

#3 Allow for Competition

Boys Need Motivation to Learn

Boys thrive on competition! It's not just something they enjoy—it's an essential part of how they learn and grow. When boys have the opportunity to compete, their learning accelerates. Competition drives them to push themselves, sharpen their skills, and test their limits. It taps into their natural desire to prove themselves and encourages them to go beyond what they thought was possible.

Competition goes beyond just winning or losing—it's about challenging oneself to be better, work harder, and achieve goals. When handled correctly, competition can be a powerful motivator, fueling ambition and reinforcing a growth mindset. Through this, boys learn that effort and perseverance lead to improvement, and they begin to embrace challenges as opportunities rather than obstacles.

While many classrooms have moved away from competitive activities to protect self-esteem and prevent arguments and hurt feelings, this shift has actually done boys a disservice. For many boys, healthy competition doesn't harm confidence—it builds it up. Rather than causing anxiety, competition motivates boys to rise to the occasion, developing perseverance and self-worth. When structured properly, it becomes a catalyst for learning and a tool for building strong character. Boys often see it not as pressure but as an opportunity.

Fostering Healthy Competition for Boys

Boys need activities with a clear outcome. Phrases like "Everyone's a winner," or "It doesn't matter who won," rarely motivate. Without real stakes, many boys will quickly lose interest. Games and activities without clearly defined goals feel empty and pointless.

Boys show incredible drive when there's something to strive for—a reward, recognition, or even just the thrill of victory. If games begin with "it doesn't matter who wins," a boy's natural intensity will fade a little. They need to feel the stakes to fully engage. Even if it's just proving to themselves that they could do it, it still matters.

If you've ever struggled with behavior issues in the classroom, a lack of competition could be an underlying cause. Without structured challenges to focus on, boys can quickly become bored. And when boredom sets in, they create their own challenges—which could become disruptive and often inappropriate. Without a proper outlet, a boy's competitive energy often turns into misbehavior, leading to frustration and discipline issues.

The solution is simple: establish a structured, competitive environment that is both engaging and motivating. It's not about turning every activity into a contest; it's about providing meaningful competitive opportunities that challenge boys and give them goals to strive for. With creativity and intentional planning, you can keep boys engaged, harness their competitive spirit, and turn learning into something productive. Done right, this approach can also reduce behavior problems by channeling boys' energy into positive outcomes, helping them develop skills like teamwork, perseverance, and sportsmanship.

Building Up Weakness and Keeping Competition Healthy

Something that needs to be addressed when talking about competition is what happens after a loss. In sports or any other games, boys will often blame someone else for the loss. If that blame isn't true, shut it down quickly and have them move on.

However, when the blame has an element of truth to it, it's okay to acknowledge that one boy may not be good at something and is dragging the rest of the team down. In those moments, turn it into an opportunity for a stronger boy to help the one who is struggling. This isn't a time to mask the truth or avoid saying what needs to be said just because it might hurt feelings. Sometimes the reality is that one player really is making things harder for the group.

Instead of complaining about the weaker player, boys need to learn to encourage and build him up. Maybe they need to push themselves harder to make up for the loss. These are real-life lessons. In the real world, some people are weaker, and others have to pick up the slack.

Be careful not to sugarcoat problems, but also address them with kindness and measured strength. Much like doctors are trained not to lie or give false reassurance, we shouldn't avoid acknowledging how bad something is. Boys need to learn that balance: building others up while still keeping a healthy sense of reality.

Sometimes a simple change helps. Switching up arguing partners, mixing teams, or giving boys who have been blaming each other a second chance to win together can defuse tension. Set them up for a shared success at something you know they can handle. That builds confidence and repairs relationships.

When one boy is repeatedly underperforming or being excluded, give him clear, specific tasks for improvement and chances to practice privately or in smaller groups. Praise effort and progress more than innate ability. That approach helps weaker players grow without shame—and it teaches stronger players leadership and patience.

Practical Strategies for Incorporating Competition

Ahead are strategies that have been successfully used to foster a healthy, competitive classroom where boys stay motivated, engaged, and empowered to succeed. I encourage talking with other teachers and exploring new ideas and ways to encourage competition in the classroom.

A. Games and Events

Structured games are one of the best ways to focus boys' competitive energy. Whether it's academic challenges like spelling bees and math relays, or physical games like obstacle courses and Rock-Paper-Scissors, competition adds excitement and drive.

Events like scavenger hunts or trivia contests encourage strategy and teamwork. Be sure to establish a clear winner and celebrate the win—because it matters.

 Tips:

1. Don't overuse favorite games—take a break and bring the game back after a while.

2. If a student takes competition too seriously, remind them it's just a game, and not to get too carried away—this is a learning opportunity.

B. Mix Up Teams

A great way to keep competition healthy and productive is by regularly randomizing teams. This encourages fairness, builds social connections, and reduces rivalry. Boys learn to work with a range of classmates and focus on the challenge and team spirit rather than on an individual friend. When students don't know who they'll be paired with next, they are more likely to cooperate with different classmates, promoting inclusivity and reducing tension between competitors.

Frequent rotation keeps the experience fresh, prevents predictable rivalries, and allows students to develop new connections. While some competitive energy may linger after a game or activity, be sure to channel this energy positively, leaving students motivated rather than frustrated.

In some cases, projects benefit from consistent teams, such as extended challenges, long-term projects, or season-based competitions. By balancing short-term and long-term team strategies during class time, students gain both adaptability and deeper investment in teamwork. The key is striking a balance—allowing competition to drive engagement while ensuring it remains a tool for growth rather than division.

Tips:

1. Boys vs girls is always a fun challenge, but try keeping things fair for both sides.

2. Randomize teams using shirt color, birth month, number of pets, or a simple coin toss. *Yes, teams may be unbalanced—this is part of the challenge.

3. Have two boys that don't get along well? Pair them together on a team and see how they come together after winning!

C. Use Everyday Challenges

Competition doesn't always need to come from a structured game or formal activity. Often, the best competitive moments are the spontaneous, everyday challenges woven naturally into classroom routines. These small, fun challenges don't require elaborate planning—they can be seamlessly integrated into tasks students are already doing. The key is recognizing opportunities to inject energy and motivation into daily activities through friendly rivalry.

For example, cleaning up can become a race: "Who can clean up their desk the fastest?" Or even, "Who can get their desk the cleanest?" Speed doesn't always have to be the challenge—quality or quantity can be factors as well. Lining up can be turned into a quick challenge: "Let's see which row can line up the quietest." Even transitioning between subjects can be made more engaging: with a playful tone, "Who thinks they can get their materials ready before I do?" These simple additions turn routine tasks into challenging opportunities, encouraging students to stay focused while having fun.

Beyond physical tasks, competition can also be embedded into academics. Quick-response challenges, such as "Who can correctly answer this math problem first?" or "Who can name the most state capitals in one minute?" encourage sharp thinking and active participation. These types of challenges are particularly effective for boys, as they thrive on moments where they can test their knowledge and skills in real time.

Nearly any situation—whether it's answering a question, completing a task, or following a procedure—can be transformed into an opportunity for healthy competition. By consistently weaving these moments into the classroom culture, you keep students motivated, focused, and excited about learning. Over time, these small competitive interactions make lessons more engaging and help students develop resilience, teamwork, and the ability to work under pressure.

Tips:

1. Let students come up with some of the challenges. This increases their investment and creativity.

2. Throw in the occasional "impossible challenge" just for laughs—like naming every student in the room in just 5 seconds. *This also falls under section 7# Allow More Humor and Goofiness.*

3. Avoid using competition as a tool just to make them work. They can tell you're just trying to get them to do work and will lose interest.

D. Personal Challenges Within Academics

While academic achievement can play a role in competition, it shouldn't be the main focus. Boys usually thrive in physical and interactive challenges that match their energy and need for movement. Since much of their day already revolves around academics, piling on more academic competition often isn't as effective. The more physical the challenge, the better.

That said, some boys need greater academic challenge to stay engaged. If a student finishes quickly and grows restless, or if he struggles to start because the work feels too easy, it may be time to raise the bar. Instead of letting boredom lead to getting off task, offer advanced work or enrichment tasks that push him to think more deeply.

You don't always need brand-new assignments—just increase the challenge. For example: "How much of this page can you memorize in 10 minutes?" or "Can you find patterns between these math problems?" These tweaks turn routine work into stimulating tasks that demand focus and creativity.

Many boys will even create their own challenges. I once had a high schooler try to prove mathematically that zero equaled one. His theory was a stretch, but he poured himself into it and walked away with a deeper grasp of math than any standard lesson could have given him.

With small adjustments like these, ordinary work becomes an engaging challenge that strengthens learning while keeping boys invested.

Tips:

1. Ask students if there's anything they'd like to focus on more or ways they'd like to make the work more challenging.

2. It's okay to start with a harder challenge, then adjust if it's too much.

E. Dealing With Loss and Failure

When a boy repeatedly loses or is the weak link in a team activity, it's easy for him to become discouraged or even check out completely. He might start to believe he's just "bad" at something, or worse—that he doesn't belong. In those moments, your response matters more than you may realize. This is a prime opportunity to coach both skill and character.

So what can you do in that situation?

As teachers, we can begin by shifting the focus from outcome to effort. Avoid saying winning doesn't matter, because to boys, it does. Instead, acknowledge the importance of the activity while still highlighting what truly moves him forward. Celebrate the small wins: a better attitude, quicker response time, improved teamwork, or even a willingness to try again after a loss. Recognize measurable progress, however small, and direct the focus to the next challenge.

At the same time, help him see setbacks as part of the growth process. Talk through what went wrong, and frame it as a chance to learn rather than a permanent weakness. Sometimes, just pointing out that every athlete, leader, or classmate has faced moments of failure can help him realize he's not alone.

A little help can go a long way in building confidence, but be careful not to offer so much support that it becomes coddling or creates false hope. The goal is to keep his motivation high while preserving the challenge and sharpening—not dulling—his competitive edge. By combining encouragement with clear expectations, you're showing him that mistakes don't define him—but resilience, effort, and growth do.

Tips:

1. Try pairing him with a supportive teammate who can encourage him without taking over or criticizing.

2. Consider smaller wins by breaking bigger challenges into parts that are more achievable.

3. Encourage privately, not publicly, to protect his dignity and keep his confidence and respect intact.

In Summary

When used intentionally, competition fuels motivation, sharpens focus, and encourages boys to aim higher. A classroom that embraces healthy competition helps boys develop not only knowledge but also valuable character traits like perseverance, teamwork, and resilience. Remember, it's not as much about winning or losing (but don't tell them that), it's about rising to the challenge and finding motivation in the pursuit of growth.

Rather than resisting boys' natural drive to compete, channel it and use it. Give them meaningful challenges and opportunities to prove themselves throughout the lesson. Whether it's academic games, classroom tasks, or everyday routines, framing activities with a competitive edge keeps boys engaged and focused. When boys feel the thrill of a challenge, they come alive—and you may be amazed at how far they'll be willing to go for a good challenge.

When competition crosses the line and boys begin picking fights, it can quickly undermine teamwork and disrupt the classroom. For strategies on handling out-of-control competition, see *Coaching Boys Through Conflict With Each Other* on page 159.

Reflection Questions

1. Think back to your own school years—how did competition affect your motivation and engagement?

2. Do you notice boys in your class becoming more focused or enthusiastic when there's a clear challenge or goal?

3. How do you currently respond to competitive energy in your classroom—do you encourage it, avoid it, or redirect it?

4. Have you seen examples of unhealthy competition among your students? What contributed to that, and how did you respond?

5. What concerns do you have about introducing more competition, and what might be lost if you don't?

Application Questions

1.   Identify one classroom activity this week that could be turned into a simple competition. What outcome will make it fun and focused?

2.   Plan a short academic game that includes teams, clear rules, and a reward—try it and note how the boys respond.

3.   Pick one daily routine (lining up, transitioning, cleaning up) and frame it as a challenge—observe what changes.

4.   Choose one boy who seems bored or disengaged. What kind of competitive challenge might help re-engage him?

5.   Ask your class to help you come up with three new classroom challenges—they might surprise you with their ideas!

"When you can measure what you are speaking about, and express it in numbers, you know something about it; but when you cannot measure it... your knowledge is of a meagre and unsatisfactory kind." – Lord Kelvin

#4 Utilize Numbers and Facts

Boys Love Trivia and How Things Work

Boys are naturally drawn to raw, concrete information —things like trivia, figures, and data points. You don't even need to embellish or dramatize the facts; presenting simple facts, as they are, often sparks interest. Whether it's science, history, language, art, math, etc., incorporating statistics or tangible data helps connect with their learning style.

They're also curious about how and why things work. Boys enjoy exploring movement, understanding cause and effect, and figuring out what makes things tick. When they connect with a book or project, it's usually because it's packed with explanations, technical details, or new discoveries. Whether it's machines, natural phenomena, or technology, boys are often most drawn to the "how" and "why" behind it all.

While boys tend to be less interested in the emotional side of things and relationships, they are more likely to engage with the mechanics of an event. They want to understand how something happened and what caused it. This natural interest in structure and function makes subjects like physics, science, engineering, math, and logic-based reasoning particularly appealing.

For example, in a story about someone lost in the woods, boys are more likely to focus on how the character finds food, builds shelter, or navigates back home, rather than the feelings and emotions associated with the situation.

To engage a boy's mind, they need opportunities to analyze how things work or explore why something happens. Even better, let him explain the concept to others

—this reinforces what they learned while building confidence and communication skills.

Historical facts, record-breaking numbers, and real-world data can be integrated into nearly any subject. Incorporate statistics, comparisons, and data visualizations, and observe what your boys are naturally curious about. Whether it's sports stats, historical timelines, or scientific data, tapping into their interests helps drive deeper focus and lasting engagement.

Practical Strategies for Incorporating Numbers and Facts

By weaving raw data and trivia into your lessons, you create natural entry points for curiosity and discussion. As said before, discuss with other teachers and explore creative ways to incorporate numbers and facts into your lessons. The following ideas offer practical ways to bring this kind of content into the classroom in a way that sparks interest and deepens learning.

A. Distances and Measurements

When teaching about places, events, or objects, include physical measurements. It makes the lesson more real and easier to visualize. For example, compare the Great Wall of China's length to the distance between two familiar cities, or explain how fast the Apollo spacecraft traveled to the moon.

Adding measurements gives students better perspective and understanding. Comparing a dinosaur's size to a school bus, or lining up timelines of major events, helps boys grasp scale and sequence. It also builds critical thinking and spatial reasoning.

Tips:

1. Let students calculate the distances or sizes themselves.

2. Encourage "what if" conversations about how things could've been different if a particular number or measurement was changed.

B. Dates and Times

Using timelines, calendars, graphs, and charts helps organize information visually and logically. These tools make abstract concepts like time and sequence more concrete. They also highlight cause-and-effect relationships between events.

For example, showing how key events in history overlap or build on each other, instead of teaching them as separate, unrelated events, helps students understand more. Graphs and charts can help track trends like population growth or technological advancements.

Tips:

1. Have students create their own timelines to organize events.

2. Encourage them to notice patterns and connections in dates and times.

C. Word Usage and Sentence Patterns

Tracking how often certain words or ideas appear in a lesson can help students understand key words and themes. This also builds language awareness and strengthens reading comprehension.

For example, students could count how many times certain words like "freedom" or "energy" appear in a text. Discussing why those words are used or repeated helps students understand the message and tone an author is trying to convey.

Tips:

1. Use this as a chance to practice grammar skills (e.g., identifying nouns and verbs).

2. Explore synonyms or alternative word choices and discuss why the author chose certain words.

3. Choosing more masculine words, like the example above, versus words like "Friendship" or "Beautiful," will keep them more engaged.

D. Interesting Facts About People

Share interesting details about important figures in history like scientists, leaders, or any other famous individual. Instead of the usual information given about an individual, include personal details—such as their age, where they lived, or the tools they used. Noting birthdays or other key life events adds context and humanizes the people you are discussing. It also strengthens connections between the person's story and the lesson material.

Tips:

1. Let students research a historical figure or create a short bio on themselves.

2. Ask them to research and collect key dates or facts about someone they are studying.

E. Special Events

Major events like battles, discoveries, or anniversaries are great tools for engagement. Focus on the details—tools used, tactics employed, or strategies involved—to connect with boys' interest in action and logistics.

Boys are often fascinated by things like military strategy or the science behind large-scale events. Describing the mechanics of a battle or how new technology influenced the outcome will captivate them.

Remember to add in elements, such as casualty numbers or survival statistics. And yes, boys love to discuss types of injuries and imagine how bloody a situation might have been. They love that stuff and it is a healthy way of processing life in general.

Tips:

1. Let students act out parts of the event or recreate the strategic plan that took place.

2. Encourage creative thinking—ask what they would've done differently and why.

In Summary

Integrating facts, measurements, timelines, and raw data into your lessons taps into how many boys naturally learn. These concrete elements give them something to visualize, analyze, and explore—making abstract ideas feel more real and engaging.

Give boys opportunities to discover, build, calculate, and explain. Let them figure out how far the nearest planet is, how fast a cheetah runs, or how much a Viking sword weighed. Graphs, comparisons, and timelines spark curiosity and build confidence. Boys love to prove they know something—lean into that drive.

If you don't know an answer, turn it into a challenge: "Who can find out before tomorrow?" This kind of mission gives them ownership and a reason to care. And here's the best part: when boys are excited to learn, everything else gets easier. They focus more, participate more, and retain more—because they're not just learning about facts, they're discovering them.

Reflection Questions

1. When you think about the boys in your classroom or group, what kinds of facts or topics naturally capture their attention?

2. Are there subjects you currently teach that could be made more engaging by incorporating more data, measurements, timelines, etc.?

3. Have you observed a boy light up when learning how something works? What did that tell you about their learning style?

4. Do you tend to focus more on emotional/relational elements or mechanical/practical elements in your lessons? How might you bring more balance?

5. What barriers do you face when trying to use facts and figures in your teaching? How could you begin to overcome them?

Application Questions

1. What is one upcoming lesson where you could include measurements, statistics, or charts to enhance understanding?

2. How can you incorporate a "how things work" explanation into an existing unit or activity?

3. Choose a historical or science topic—how might you build a project around distances, timelines, or tools used?

4. What kind of fact-finding or "mini-investigation" could you assign to a student or small group this week?

5. How might you use word tracking or sentence pattern analysis to build reading comprehension in a fun, fact-focused way?

"Leaders aren't born, they are made. And they are made just like anything else–through hard work." – Vince Lombardi

#5 Encourage Leadership and Responsibility

Boys Need Leadership to Build Responsibility

Boys need opportunities to lead and take ownership of their actions. Instead of constantly directing them on what to do and how to do it, we should give them the freedom to make decisions and exercise leadership in their daily lives. This sense of autonomy fosters independence and helps boys develop essential life skills such as responsibility and sound decision-making. Leadership isn't just about leading others—it's also about personal management of tasks, making choices, and being accountable for oneself.

Encouraging boys to lead is a vital part of their personal growth. When they are entrusted with decisions, even small ones, it builds discipline and accountability. These qualities are critical not only for academic success but also for long-term maturity. The more opportunities boys have to lead, the better prepared they will be for the future—and for your classroom. Leadership builds confidence, resilience, and a sense of ownership over personal choices and behavior.

Most boys naturally enjoy doing things for themselves. If a young boy is struggling with a task—like tying his shoe —encourage him to try on his own rather than stepping in to help. Support him, but don't take over. I often see very helpful teachers, with well-meaning intentions, jump right in to help or correct students. Try allowing boys the space to problem-solve and do it on their own first. This builds competence and confidence, and is an essential step in their development.

Freedom Within Boundaries

Leadership doesn't mean unlimited freedom. Boys still need structure and boundaries. Offer them choices within clear, age-appropriate limitations. For example, instead of giving too much freedom by asking, "Which paragraph would you like to read?" try, "Would you like to read paragraph one or two?" This small adjustment empowers boys to make decisions while still keeping the class on track and accomplishing what needs to be done. Offering structured choices respects their ability to decide and teaches them how to evaluate options effectively.

Decision-making opportunities are also a powerful way to maintain engagement. Boys are more motivated when they feel they have a stake in the outcome. When given a choice, they develop a sense of ownership and are more likely to follow through. Active participation in shaping their learning experience encourages initiative and long-term investment in their education.

A key distinction between boys and girls often lies in their sense of urgency. Generally speaking, girls tend to expect a task to be completed right away, while boys often add it to a mental checklist to complete at some point. When a boy is asked to do something, he may not act immediately but still intends to follow through. For example, if a girl asks someone to clean up, she typically expects it done right then. A boy making the same request might be satisfied as long as it gets done at some point in the near future. When assigning tasks, keep this difference in mind and set clear expectations for timing.

As boys mature, the teacher's role shifts from providing constant direction to allowing more autonomy. Younger boys may need more direct structure, while older boys can take on more meaningful responsibilities like leading group discussions, managing projects, or organizing classroom activities. While the balance between freedom and structure shifts with age, the core principle remains the same: boys need to be empowered to make decisions and take the lead—while also understanding the boundaries they must respect and stay within.

Failure Needs To Be An Option

With opportunities to lead come opportunities to fail. Leadership is about more than guiding others toward success; it's also about learning from setbacks and allowing for mistakes to happen. This is a vital principle in the classroom. Teachers must be willing to allow students to make poor choices and experience the natural consequences of their actions. It may feel counterintuitive, but for boys especially, failure can be a powerful teacher.

Too often, boys are shielded from failure in an attempt to protect them. But in doing so, we deprive them of critical life experiences. Sometimes boys need to learn the hard way. Through mistakes, they build resilience, problem-solving skills, and a clearer understanding of how their actions affect others and themselves.

Obviously, this does not mean exposing boys to very dangerous or life-altering consequences. Teachers should help students navigate smaller failures in a way that encourages growth while maintaining a certain level of safety. The classroom provides an ideal setting for this kind of learning—the stakes are low, but the lessons are real.

These small setbacks, when experienced in a safe and structured environment, teach valuable life skills. Boys can explore their limits, reflect on their choices, and develop the maturity needed to face bigger challenges later in life.

Failure is not the end of the road; it's the beginning of growth. By creating safe opportunities for boys to fail, reflect, and try again, educators foster both character and competence. It's through these experiences that boys develop into strong, capable, and thoughtful young men.

Practical Strategies for Developing Leadership Skills

Ahead are practical strategies that can help boys grow in leadership and personal responsibility. These approaches encourage independence, strengthen decision-making, and help boys take ownership of their time, tasks, and behavior in a structured, supportive way. This list is not exhaustive—continue exploring new creative ways to provide leadership opportunities for boys in the classroom.

A. Time Management

Foster leadership by giving boys a voice in how they manage their time. Time management is a key life skill, and the classroom is a great place to begin developing it in a meaningful, low-stakes way. During transitions between activities, rather than abruptly saying, "Time's up, put everything away," let them know in advance how much time they have to complete the task. This gives them a framework to practice pacing themselves and to begin thinking about how to use their time wisely.

It's natural to want to offer a few extra minutes if a student is falling behind, especially if he's working hard. Nevertheless, constantly extending deadlines can be counterproductive. If boys are to learn time management, they need to experience the consequences of misjudging how long something takes. Adjusting the goalposts to make things easier may feel supportive in the moment, but it actually hinders their ability to develop personal accountability and the ability to plan ahead.

For older students, take it a step further by involving them in the time-planning process. Ask, "How much time do you think you'll need to finish this assignment?" Their initial response may be unrealistic, but that's okay—it opens the door for a conversation about setting reasonable expectations. Guide them toward a few manageable options, and once a time is agreed upon, stick to it. This reinforces the connection between their decisions and the outcomes, helping them build self-discipline and respect for boundaries.

By gradually giving boys more control over how they manage their own time—and holding them to it—you're not only teaching an important life skill; you're building confidence and responsibility.

 Tips:

1. Timers and alarms are great tools for this!

2. If you do offer extra time to finish a project, stick to that adjustment—do not extend it again.

3. Use analog clocks as helpful visuals for time keeping.

B. Classroom Responsibilities

Assigning boys simple leadership roles fosters a sense of responsibility. Some easy leadership-building tasks in a classroom could include:

- Turning the lights on and off during a video.
- Organizing classroom materials.
- Taking attendance or calling out names.
- Helping classmates resolve minor conflicts.
- Leading group activities or discussions.
- Assisting with setup or clean up after projects.
- Passing out or collecting assignments.
- Managing the classroom's technology.
- Running classroom errands.
- Helping to create and post classroom displays.
- Being a "classroom monitor."
- Leading warm-up, stretching activities or "brain-breaks."

These tasks can help develop leadership and task management skills in a low-pressure setting. If they are unable to complete an assigned task, don't give them additional chances; take the task away, and build back to it later, if appropriate.

Tips:

1. Start small, by assigning simple tasks first to build confidence before larger, more responsible ones.

2. Set clear expectations by being specific on what the job involves and what a successful outcome looks like.

3. When appropriate, let them take on bigger tasks they're interested in, even if they aren't fully ready—those moments can become powerful teaching opportunities.

C. Teaching and Peer Support

Allow boys to take part in teaching. Whether leading a discussion, presenting a part of a lesson, or helping peers, these opportunities can inspire confidence, reinforce understanding, and build communication skills. Even if it's not perfect, it's meaningful—boys thrive when they're trusted and respected. Teaching peers boosts their self-esteem and helps them feel like contributors to the learning process.

Tips:

1. Start small, by assigning simple tasks first to build confidence before larger, more responsible tasks.

2. Set clear expectations by being specific on what the job involves and what a successful outcome looks like.

3. Ask them what they might do differently if they were the ones teaching the lesson you just completed.

D. Ownership With Assignments

Giving boys a say in their assignments fosters responsibility and autonomy. Simple adjustments can make a big difference, such as allowing them to choose between topics or presentation formats.

With freedom comes responsibility. If a student takes a lazy or humorous approach that lacks substance, guide them in understanding the balance between creativity and meeting expectations. Hold them accountable for their choices, reinforcing the idea that effort directly influences results. If they are dissatisfied with a grade due to their lack of effort, remind them politely that they made the choice to complete the assignment in such a manner. This reinforces personal accountability and the consequences of their decisions while encouraging them to improve in the future.

About Younger Students

For younger students, ownership of assignments can look different but still be effective. For example:

- Let them choose to read aloud in a voice of their choosing; Batman voice or a robot voice.
- Allow them to pick between writing about a pirate ship or a space adventure.
- Have them use their snack to help count numbers for math problems.

These simple options create positive associations with learning, encouraging autonomy while maintaining structure.

Note: When given the freedom to be creative, boys will most likely include monsters, swords, and graphic battles in their creative work—this is normal and reflects their natural language. This should not be discouraged—as long as it doesn't get too carried away—as it supports storytelling and engagement using their natural voice and style. Unfortunately, many teachers feel violent scenarios are inappropriate for the classroom, but this is the natural language of boys and should not be discouraged. More is said on this matter in the next section, *#6 Use Masculine Language.*

In Summary

Giving boys leadership over their actions and decisions enhances their academic experience while preparing them for adulthood. This kind of responsibility goes beyond simply managing classroom tasks—it shapes character. By trusting boys with real choices, whether small or significant, you communicate that their contributions matter. Over time, this builds ownership and pride in their work.

The process naturally develops life skills like critical thinking, responsibility, and initiative. Boys begin to weigh consequences before acting, consider how their choices affect others, and recognize that leadership is as much about service as it is about authority. Even when they make mistakes—and they will—those moments become valuable lessons in resilience, humility, and problem-solving.

Fostering leadership doesn't only give boys control— it's about creating opportunities to make decisions, learn from failures, and grow in maturity. Leadership in the classroom might look like leading a group project, mentoring a younger student, or helping manage class routines. Each of these experiences gives them a chance to practice influence in a safe, supportive environment.

When boys feel empowered, they are more likely to become confident, capable, and resilient young men— ready to lead in and beyond the classroom. What starts with a simple opportunity to step up can echo into the rest of their lives, shaping them into husbands, fathers, workers, and citizens who lead with strength and wisdom.

You may be surprised by how dramatically a so-called "problem" student's behavior can change when he's given the chance to lead. Boys who often challenge authority or push boundaries are frequently the same ones with natural leadership potential—they just haven't yet learned how to direct it in positive ways. When trusted with responsibility, these boys often rise to the occasion, showing focus, initiative, and pride in earning that trust. What once looked like defiance can transform into determination when they realize their energy and influence can make a real difference.

Reflection Questions

1. In what ways do I currently allow boys in my classroom to take the lead?

2. Do I tend to step in too quickly when a boy struggles, or do I allow room for problem-solving and growth?

3. How comfortable am I with letting boys fail at something? Why or why not?

4. What beliefs or habits might be holding me back from giving boys more autonomy in decision-making?

5. How do I balance structure and freedom in my teaching or leadership style?

Application Questions

1. What is one classroom responsibility I can delegate to a particular boy to build leadership skills?

2. How can I incorporate more structured choices into my daily interactions with boys?

3. What opportunities can I create for boys to teach, present, or lead their peers?

4. What small, safe opportunities for failure can I allow—followed by reflection and guidance?

5. How can I adjust my expectations and communication style to better align with how boys process and respond to instructions or timing?

"We don't see things as they are; we see them as we are." – Anaïs Nin

#6 Use Masculine Language

Boys Engage Through Masculine Language

While this entire book focuses on engaging boys through masculine language, this section takes a closer look at the practical side: the actual words you use, communication styles, and the design of your classroom environment. Together, these elements create a space where boys feel connected, motivated, and ready to learn.

Many teachers are trained to use gentle, nurturing language in the classroom. This approach—often more feminine in nature—certainly helps create warmth, safety, and a supportive atmosphere, but it isn't always the most effective way to reach boys. Boys tend to respond more positively to communication that is direct, firm, action-oriented, and strong.

Think about how members of a military unit or a sports team interact. Their communication carries strength; it is clear, assertive, and purposeful. They don't rely on cautious or overly affectionate tones. Instead, they speak with confidence, call out weaknesses directly, and push one another to improve. Their words may sound blunt or harsh at times, yet they carry conviction, urgency, and strength—qualities that naturally resonate with boys. Speaking the language of boys means using words with authority, clarity, and respect—communication that conveys purpose and expectation.

Boys thrive on firm, straightforward, and challenging language. They stay engaged when spoken to with authority and called to a higher standard. Don't be fooled by their cute, innocent faces—many boys are rough around the edges and respond best to strong, purposeful words that command them to rise up and meet a challenge.

That's not to say boys shouldn't hear gentle language—they absolutely need gentle encouragement and can be built up through a tender, nurturing voice. What's emphasized here is that boys naturally gravitate toward strength and masculine tones. Overly soft or excessively kind language—though well-intentioned and appropriate at times—may not always be the best approach. Speaking with a commanding masculine presence reaches the deepest part of a boy's inner man, inviting action and inspiring respect.

When we speak to boys with strength, we communicate respect—and respect is the foundation of connection. This same principle applies not only to what we say, but how we say it. The tone, phrasing, and style of our speech all send a message about how much we believe in a boy's capability and maturity.

Avoiding Childish Speech

Teachers sometimes use exaggerated tones, overly simplified language, or third-person instructions like, "We don't do that here" or "We raise our hands when we want to talk." While these phrases are well-intentioned, they can come across as condescending—especially to boys, who notice that adults don't speak this way to each other. Instead, use normal, strong tones, proper words, and clear instructions. Speak with respect, as if addressing another adult.

Another aspect of childish speech is repeating or reinforcing incorrect words students use. Even if a mispronunciation sounds cute, it still needs correction. For example, if a young child says "lellow" instead of "yellow," model the correct pronunciation rather than echoing the incorrect one.

Some speech patterns—while not necessarily childish—tend to sound more feminine, such as adding an "-ee" sound to words (e.g., "doggy" instead of "dog," "mommy" instead of "mom"). There's nothing inherently wrong with these words, but when your goal is to speak the language of boys, it's important to choose strong, direct, and straightforward language, without making it sound "cute."

The same applies to compliments. Phrases like "You look so cute" or "That outfit is adorable" may feel natural, but they don't resonate with boys the way they might with girls. Boys respond better to words like "cool," "sharp," or "awesome," which affirm their identity in a way that conveys strength and masculinity. Speaking to boys with strength rather than cutesy speech takes practice—but they will notice and respect you for treating them as capable, maturing young men.

Create a Space That Speaks Their Language

Your classroom's physical environment communicates just as much as your words. Boys are observant—they read tone, body language, and décor.

Look around your classroom: Are the walls coated in pastel colors or decorated with butterflies, flowers, hearts, or soft textures? Are colorful rugs and cozy pillows the dominant features? Have you included scents reminiscent of a craft, candle, or soap store?

While these touches may feel warm and inviting— especially for female students—they can feel feminine and out of place for many boys. Think about how many grown men avoid spaces that feel overly feminine. Now imagine how much more this can affect young boys.

Boys are often drawn to environments that signal action, challenge, and adventure. Sometimes this simply means fewer distractions—less color, less clutter, more open space. Think of a fire station, a military barracks, or a wide-open gym. These spaces aren't designed to be cozy— they are purposeful, practical, and built for movement. This is the type of environment boys want and need.

Spaces that may feel plain or empty to girls often feel exciting and freeing to boys, allowing them room to run, jump, wrestle, climb, and test their strength. Even settings that feel rough—or even slightly unsafe—to girls can be where boys feel most alive and engaged.

To be clear, no one is suggesting you turn your classroom into a bunker or fire house—but a few simple changes can make it more boy-friendly. Use bold, grounded colors like navy, charcoal, or earth tones. Choose visuals that convey energy: sports, exploration, machines, dangerous creatures, or landscapes. Decor that reflects strength and movement helps boys feel grounded and ready to learn.

Villains, Battles, Aliens, and Monsters

Teachers will often gravitate toward stories and assignments that emphasize beauty, relationships, harmony, and emotional depth. While these themes are meaningful, boys often approach storytelling through a different lens.

Boys are naturally drawn to action, conflict, conquest, and destruction. Pirate battles, alien invasions, sea monsters, sword fights, and hero-versus-villain scenarios are developmentally normal. Drawing beheaded soldiers, sketching violent battles, or discussing epic conflicts may sound shocking, but for many boys, this is how their imagination works.

It can feel uncomfortable for educators who view such content as violent or inappropriate because it differs from how most teachers approach these subjects. However, this is how boys process details, explore courage, and wrestle with questions of justice and power. Suppressing these interests can backfire—boys may feel alienated or misunderstood or learn to hide and bottle up their true feelings.

Allowing boys to explore imaginative violence and intense action is healthy and supports growth. Whether through writing, drawing, conversation, or acting, these outlets foster emotional development, engagement, creativity, and a confident, authentic voice.

That said, it's essential to distinguish between healthy expression and signs of emotional distress. A vivid battlefield story differs from repeated writing or artwork centered on self-harm, despair, or hopelessness—especially with real-world references, isolation, or feelings of being trapped. When creative work becomes unusually dark, or a student appears withdrawn, angry, or detached, this behavior warrants attention. Such signs may indicate deeper struggles like depression, anxiety, or harmful thinking, and must always be taken seriously.

At the same time, boys often use dramatic, intense imagery as part of normal creative expression. Writing stories with villains' heads blown to pieces, drawing bloody soldiers, or explosions is developmentally appropriate—at any age really. Recognizing this as normal allows teachers to support boys without unnecessarily restricting their imagination, while remaining alert for real emotional concerns.

The key is creating a classroom culture where boys can express bold, sometimes violent ideas while maintaining clear boundaries. For example: "It's okay to include battles in your story—but we need to see what your hero learns or overcomes in the end." Encouraging themes of redemption, growth, and justice alongside action validates boys' interests while guiding them toward healthy reflection.

Fostering open conversations and trust also helps boys discuss real-life issues when needed. Teaching emotional language and coping strategies alongside storytelling enables them to distinguish fantasy from reality.

Ultimately, giving boys space to be themselves—while monitoring who they are becoming—is one of the most powerful ways teachers can support masculine growth, both creatively and emotionally.

Masculine Kindness

When we talk about kindness, love, and compassion, we often imagine soft, gentle expressions. While these traits are important, they are often emphasized in ways that are more feminine. Boys respond better to kindness in a context that is more masculine—where strength and care work together.

Kindness doesn't always look gentle. It can show through standing firm, protecting others, or challenging someone for their own good. When a boy defends a friend from bullying, he demonstrates courage, assertiveness, and a willingness to be uncomfortable. That is kindness through strength—bold, purposeful, and protective.

Helping a loved one struggling with addiction requires emotional toughness—setting firm boundaries even when it's painful. A leader taking responsibility for a team's failure—shielding others from harm—is another form of strength expressed as care.

Masculine kindness often shows up in action, problem-solving, and protection. A mentor might not offer comforting words but will step in with practical support, solutions, or playful humor. Strong mentors lead by example, showing resilience, discipline, and quiet sacrifice.

Even encouragement can be framed through action. Pushing a friend or student to exceed their limits—out of belief in their potential—is a form of care through strength. Boys need to see and internalize this masculine model of compassion. Consider how boys and girls play with younger children. Girls often let younger kids win; boys play hard, expecting others to rise to the challenge. Neither is wrong—but boys show care by pushing others to grow, not by holding back.

Teaching boys how their natural drive for strength can be used for kindness helps them understand that masculinity and goodness are compatible. They simply need to channel their energy to protect, encourage, and support others.

Special Note for Female Educators

These strategies don't diminish the qualities you already bring—warmth, nurturing, and relational skills are essential. Instead, they provide complementary tools. Just as learning key phrases in a student's native language helps with connection, incorporating masculine communication allows you to reach boys who respond best to direct, purposeful, and action-oriented language.

Your classroom doesn't need less of your natural style —it needs both feminine and masculine elements. Pairing warmth and care with clarity, firmness, and energetic guidance creates a balanced environment where all students thrive. Boys benefit from seeing models of strength and empathy, learning that compassion takes many forms. By blending approaches, you honor your teaching voice while meeting diverse student needs.

Practical Strategies for Including Masculine Language

Strong language doesn't happen by accident. Boys benefit from deliberate, action-driven communication that respects their developing sense of strength and identity. These strategies offer practical ways to shift your language to reflect a more masculine approach.

A. Speech and Tone

Sometimes it's about tone and sometimes it's about the actual words you use. Even a simple word change or how you say something can make a big difference.

- Use Direct and Confident Speech

    Instead of: "Okay, sweetie, let's try our best on this worksheet, okay?"

Try: "Alright, let's tackle this worksheet. Show me what you've got!"

This small shift sets a more confident, action-oriented tone, helping boys approach the task with excitement and determination. This approach also eliminates uncertainty.

- Incorporate Action-Oriented Words

    Instead of: "Let's quietly sit and listen."

    Try: "Attention everyone! Lock in and focus."

Words like "lock in" and "attention" frame learning as a mission, appealing to boys' natural instincts for action and competition. It also commands attention so they now know to stop what they are doing.

- Use Stronger Praise and Challenges

    Instead of: "Great job, honey! That was so nice!"

    Try: "That was solid work! I knew you could do it!"

Stronger, action-based praise acknowledges effort and achievement in a way that aligns with boys' desire to prove themselves.

- Frame Learning as an Adventure

    Instead of: "Today, we're going to read a story"

    Try: "Today, we're diving into a story—you won't believe what happens!"

Presenting lessons as exciting challenges helps to get boys excited about the work they are about to do. Plus, adding in a little mystery often draws people in.

Tips:

1. It is possible to use a calm and gentle tone while still delivering words that are strong, clear, and purposeful.

2. Try to sound natural and not like you're trying too hard.

B. A Space That Signals Strength and Purpose

Classroom environment has a powerful influence on boys' engagement and sense of identity. To encourage action and focus, replace overly decorative or "cute" elements with visuals that appeal to adventure and challenge—posters of explorers, athletes, tools, mountains, or machinery communicate movement, achievement, and purpose.

Color schemes are also important and reinforce a message; strong, grounded tones like army green, navy blue, or earthy browns create a sense of stability and seriousness. Consider adding a "challenge board" where boys can celebrate accomplishments, take on tasks, or track goals. Balance decorative elements thoughtfully: if one bulletin board is bright, flowery, colorful, and artistic, complement it with a plain, structured display—such as a "Challenge of the Week" or a goal tracker—to show that action and focus matter as much as aesthetics.

 Tips:

1. Rotate challenges weekly to keep boys engaged and provide opportunities for success.

2. Include interactive elements like checklists or goal trackers to let boys actively participate in the classroom environment.

3. Ask students for input on the mission board—they will take more ownership if they help design it.

C. Incorporate Masculine Role Models

Boys benefit from seeing diverse examples of male strength and character. Bring in books, stories, or biographies that feature men who demonstrate courage, sacrifice, leadership, and creativity. Highlight the many forms strength can take: physical strength (athletes, warriors), moral strength (whistleblowers, peacemakers), intellectual strength (inventors, strategists), and emotional strength (fathers, mentors, first responders).

Whenever possible, invite male role models to the classroom—firefighters, veterans, coaches, or dads—to share their experiences, read stories, or lead activities. These real-life connections make abstract qualities like courage and perseverance tangible and relatable.

Tips:

1. Create a rotating selection of books or stories featuring male heroes from different backgrounds and fields.

2. Discuss the different ways boys can show strength in everyday life, reinforcing that it is not only physical.

D. Celebrate Strength Through Character

Recognizing positive behavior reinforces the qualities we want boys to develop. Celebrate actions such as standing up for someone, taking responsibility for a mistake, showing initiative, or persevering through challenges. Visual recognition helps reinforce these behaviors: create a "Wall of Strength" or a "Leadership Spotlight" where boys who demonstrate courage, problem-solving, or kindness through action are highlighted. By connecting strength to character, boys learn that true courage and leadership involve both action and integrity.

Tips:

1. Encourage boys to nominate peers for recognition, fostering a culture of encouragement and awareness.

2. Use specific praise that highlights the behavior, not just the outcome (e.g., "I noticed how you helped your classmate without being asked").

3. Rotate the spotlight regularly and include girls, so all students have a chance to be recognized for different strengths.

In Summary

Boys respond to environments and communication that reflect strength, purpose, and action. By intentionally using more masculine language—and making thoughtful adjustments to your classroom design—you align your teaching with the way boys naturally engage and learn. This doesn't mean removing warmth or care; it simply means adding more firmness and strength.

The goal isn't to silence the female voice but to reintroduce the male one, creating balance. A classroom shaped by both masculine and feminine influences becomes a space where all students feel seen, valued, and challenged to grow. When boys experience an environment that reflects both strength and care, they feel more connected and focused. Incorporating masculine language and design isn't about changing who you are as a teacher—it's about expanding your reach and strengthening your impact.

By shaping your words, tone, and environment to speak the language of boys, you help them thrive academically, emotionally, and socially. And in doing so, you help raise the kind of young men our world needs.

Reflection Questions

1. How does the language used in your classroom currently impact your boys' engagement? Can you identify areas where language could be more firm or action-oriented?

2. Reflect on your classroom's design: Are there areas that might feel more welcoming or engaging to boys by incorporating dynamic visuals?

3. How does your physical environment encourage or discourage active participation and focus?

4. How does your current approach to praise reflect boys' action-oriented nature? Could feedback be more assertive or challenge-based?

5. Would adopting a more direct, confident communication style affect your classroom atmosphere? How might it help or hinder relationships with students?

Application Questions

1. What changes can you make to classroom language to better engage boys? Consider replacing softer phrases with action-oriented language.

2. Which classroom element or space could you redesign this month to appeal more to boys?

3. Choose an upcoming lesson and reframe it to be more masculine. Observe your boys' response.

4. Identify one behavior pattern possibly related to the environment. What adjustments could improve it?

5. After implementing direct speech and action-oriented phrases, how can you assess boys' responses? What observations indicate success?

"A day without laughter is a day wasted."
— Charlie Chaplin

#7 Permit Humor and Goofiness

Boys Thrive on Humor and Goofiness

Humor is at the heart of how boys communicate, bond, and process the world around them. Whether it's cracking jokes, using potty humor, acting goofy, or engaging in playful sarcastic banter, humor is—if not the—fundamental part of their social interactions. It's not only for fun—it's a tool for coping with stress, making connections, and navigating life's challenges. This is why boys will often joke in serious situations. It's their way of understanding, processing, and expressing themselves—and sometimes to help lighten the mood.

Understanding boys' natural inclination toward humor helps create a more inviting and effective learning environment. When humor is welcomed and even woven into teaching, it can transform the classroom from a rigid space into one that feels open, welcoming, and enjoyable. For many boys, humor provides what soft cushions, gentle colors, and a warm, cozy atmosphere often provide for girls: a sense of comfort, safety, and belonging. While some students relax in nurturing environments, boys often find that same connection and ease through laughter and joking around. Humor softens the edges of the classroom, breaks down tension, and makes learning feel approachable.

It's important to understand that "boy humor" often looks very different from "girl humor." When boys joke, it often involves exaggeration, something physical, witty absurdity, or playful insults. To girls, this feels childish and out of place. This difference in humor runs both ways—an interesting dynamic exists between boys and girls: each often sees the other's silliness as childish. A girl might think boys' jokes are immature, while a boy may find girls' giggling silly and childish. Neither style of humor is wrong —they're just different.

This misunderstanding can sometimes create friction. Girls roll their eyes at boyish antics, and boys scoff at girlish jokes. But these reactions often come from looking through their own lens, not from actual maturity differences. Recognizing this helps teachers mediate misunderstandings and build empathy between students— while also validating the way others use humor.

Teasing: Bonding or Bullying?

One common misunderstanding in humor among boys is teasing. A boy says he's getting a baseball award, and his friend replies, "I didn't know they gave trophies to losing teams." To an outsider, that might sound mean—but between boys, it's often a sign of friendship. Teasing, ribbing, and playful jabs are how many boys bond and communicate. The key is that it's mutual, lighthearted, and understood.

So how can you tell the difference between playful teasing and hurtful bullying? If both boys are laughing and still getting along, it's harmless fun. If one boy seems a little hurt in the moment but stays engaged, it may have gone a bit too far, but not bullying—something to watch, not necessarily stop. But if a boy repeatedly seems upset, withdraws, and reacts aggressively, a line has been crossed. Teachers should stay alert and step in when teasing becomes one-sided or persistent, while still leaving room for boys to poke fun at each other—it's part of how they connect and communicate.

The examples above apply to boys joking with boys. Boys also need to understand that girls don't always joke the same way. If a boy teases a girl and she doesn't respond well, it doesn't necessarily mean he's bullying her—it may simply mean he's treating her like one of the boys. He may not realize that's not her way of joking, especially if they're friends and he's joked with her before. Boys must learn that not everyone shares their style of humor, and they need to recognize when joking is appropriate and when it's not.

Teachers must be careful not to confuse genuine bullying with ordinary joking. Labeling innocent boyish humor as bullying not only minimizes the seriousness of real bullying but also damages boys' confidence and self-esteem.

Teaching the Boundaries of Humor

Of course, humor works best when it's used wisely. One of the most important lessons boys can learn is that timing and context matter. The key is helping them understand when humor fits—and when it doesn't. This isn't about instantly shutting down their natural playfulness, but rather guiding them to become more socially aware and emotionally intelligent.

Part of growing up is learning to "read the room." Boys often use humor to process big feelings—grief, stress, anxiety, or even embarrassment. It's not unusual for them to crack a joke during a serious moment, not to be disrespectful, but as a way to deflect discomfort or ease emotional tension. While that impulse may be healthy for them, they need help in recognizing how it might come across to others. What feels like comic relief to them may feel rude or inappropriate to someone who is hurting or trying to be serious.

That's why it's essential to teach boys when to use humor appropriately and where and with whom. If they need to make light of a tough situation, help them understand it's best done in private—with trusted friends who understand their intent—not in front of a grieving classmate, a frustrated teacher, or during a solemn moment. This kind of discernment is a life skill, and learning it early will serve them well in friendships, school, and eventually the workplace.

Teachers play a major role in this development. Boys are watching to see what makes us laugh—and what doesn't. When we model a healthy balance—laughing when it's appropriate and gently redirecting when it's not—we show them that humor has its place. You don't have to call them out harshly every time a joke misses the mark. Sometimes a simple look, pause, or quiet word after class can make a bigger impact than public correction. With that said, sometimes public correction is necessary, especially when it crosses the line of respecting a person or authority.

The goal is not to stifle their humor, but to help them mature in it. Boys don't need less humor—they need better humor. They need the tools to know when to speak, when to hold back, and how to adjust their words based on who's in the room and what's happening around them. When they learn these skills, they not only become funnier—they become more thoughtful, more empathetic, and more aware of how they impact the people around them.

Stepping Into Their World

One of the best ways to build rapport with boys is by being a little goofy yourself. Humor makes you more approachable, puts students at ease, and makes room for creativity. Boys, especially, are drawn to teachers who can laugh, play along, and not take themselves too seriously. That doesn't mean the classroom becomes a comedy show —but a well-timed joke or playful moment can go a long way.

Not all humor works—and not all attempts land well. Boys appreciate cleverness, quick wit, and humor that connects to real interests. Forced jokes or overly childish antics can fall flat, especially with older boys. Over-relying on silly voices, props, or exaggerated behavior might seem engaging, but boys can easily sense when it's insincere or patronizing.

To better understand the practical nature of humor in a classroom, I'd like to share this short example.

A mentor of mine was working with a group of middle schoolers at an event that included several rising sixth graders. Before the new students arrived, he instructed the existing students to react to the story he was going to share: laugh when he said "kidney beans" and fall out of their chairs when he said "baked beans."

When the new students arrived, he told the story. Naturally, they had no idea what was happening as everyone started laughing and falling out of their chairs. Afterwards, he explained the story and shared that this was a tradition for welcoming new students. By including them in the explanation, the new students instantly became part of the group.

This clever use of humor helped the new students feel included, creating a shared experience and an inside joke that connected everyone in that moment. This example illustrates how inside jokes and shared experiences can build relationships, establish trust, and help everyone feel connected and part of the classroom.

Use humor to complement your teaching—not just to entertain. The example above shows how humor can enhance the classroom experience rather than distract from it. Effective humor is relevant, timely, and grounded in genuine connection. Humor works best when it comes from a place of confidence, respect, and shared understanding.

Practical Strategies for Using Humor Effectively

Always be exploring more creative ways to connect with boys through humor. Ask around, be observant of the humor your boys are using, and have fun! To use humor in a way that engages boys while also teaching them when and where it's appropriate, consider the following strategies:

A. Model the Right Kind of Humor

Boys learn by example. When they see an adult using humor to enhance communication rather than distract from it, they begin to understand its power. Your attitude toward humor sets the tone for the whole class. If you use it carelessly, they'll do the same. But if you model humor that is lighthearted, respectful, and well-timed, boys will begin to see it as a tool for building connection, not just getting laughs. Demonstrate how to inject fun into discussions while still maintaining respect. In doing so, you show them that humor has boundaries and purpose—it can add to the moment without taking over.

 Tips:

1. Share funny (but appropriate) personal stories that connect to the lesson.

2. Use quick-witted responses that show you're listening and engaged.

3. Smile often and laugh with students, not at them.

4. Use gentle sarcasm or irony to show how humor can be smart and clever.

5. Point out when humor crosses the line and show how to redirect it.

B. Set Clear Expectations

Boys need to know that humor is welcome in the right context but shouldn't derail a lesson. Set clear guidelines for when humor is appropriate, helping them learn the balance between fun and focus. Don't hesitate to call a student out if their joke distracts and interrupts the class.

When this happens, my go-to line is, "Did that help the situation?" After they answer no, I follow up with, "Then why did you do it?" And close with, "Please don't do that again," and, when needed, I explain the reason behind it so they understand. This is an example of calling out in public, as it shows disrespect to the one teaching.

Tips:

1. Begin the school year by explaining the difference between helpful and harmful humor.

2. Designate times for playful moments (e.g., "fun breaks" or "joke of the day").

3. Use a visual signal (like a hand motion or bell) to redirect the class when things get too silly.

4. Reinforce that humor must never come at the expense of others' dignity and must respect others and authority.

5. Emphasize that students can be funny and focused at the same time.

C. Encourage and Reinforce Positive Humor

Some humor builds connections, while other humor alienates. Boys often test boundaries with their jokes, and part of our role as teachers is to guide them toward humor that uplifts rather than tears down. That doesn't mean shutting down every silly or sarcastic comment, but it does mean helping them recognize the difference between humor that strengthens relationships and humor that damages them. Teach boys to avoid humor that is mean-spirited, crude, or excessively immature, while still allowing space for playful teasing when it's mutual and lighthearted. By encouraging humor that adds to the learning environment and strengthens friendships, you create a classroom culture where laughter is both welcomed and safe.

Equally important is reinforcing moments when boys get it right. When a student successfully uses humor to enhance a discussion or lesson without undermining it, acknowledge it. Positive reinforcement helps them see the impact of their words, guiding them toward a mature, respectful, and effective sense of humor. Celebrating these moments shows boys that humor can be both fun and purposeful and encourages others to follow suit, fostering a classroom where playful, clever humor is valued and safe for everyone.

Tips:

1. Create classroom games or activities that require team-based humor (e.g., group skits or joke challenges).

2. Praise students for clever, kind, or constructive humor.

3. Privately thank students for helping keep the tone light and appropriate.

4. Invite students to share their joke or humorous moment again during lesson wrap-ups.

5. Consider giving a "Comedian" recognition for students who uplift others with humor.

6. Encourage boys who normally struggle with focus but engage through humor, showing them that their contributions matter.

D. Playful Exaggeration

Exaggeration is a powerful tool for engaging boys and making abstract or challenging ideas more relatable. By stretching reality just a little, you can grab attention, spark curiosity, and make lessons more memorable. This can include a bit of playful teasing, as long as it's done respectfully and never at a student's expense. Exaggeration also allows boys to see learning as fun and approachable, turning abstract concepts into stories, challenges, or scenarios they can easily picture. It encourages creativity, invites participation, and provides an outlet for energy and humor in the classroom, while keeping the focus on learning. When used thoughtfully, playful exaggeration can make both instruction and classroom interactions more lively, engaging, and memorable.

Tips:

1. Turn mistakes or misunderstandings into a little sarcasm. For example, "I like *angels* too, but I think *angles* would work better for this situation."

2. Use wildly exaggerated analogies, "This backpack is heavier than a baby elephant!".

3. Describe concepts in cartoonish or superhero terms, "Today's lesson? Defeating the evil Math Super Villain!"

4. Pretend to forget obvious simple facts about something and let students "outsmart" you. Like incorrectly calling something the wrong color or name.

E. Lighthearted Goofiness

Silliness, when purposeful, can make learning more enjoyable, memorable, and engaging for boys. Goofiness captures attention, lowers anxiety, and makes the classroom feel like a safe space to take risks, answer questions, or try something new. Boys are naturally drawn to playful behavior, and incorporating humor and lighthearted antics into lessons can turn ordinary tasks into exciting experiences. When used thoughtfully, goofiness reinforces learning, strengthens classroom relationships, and helps boys connect with material in a way that feels fun rather than forced. It also shows that learning doesn't always have to be serious—teachers can model joy, curiosity, and creativity alongside instruction, making lessons stick in ways traditional approaches may not.

Tips:

1. Use dramatic voices or accents to read text aloud.

2. Let boys "rename" boring materials, like calling a grammar worksheet "The Sentence Gauntlet."

3. Start class with a goofy riddle or "Would You Rather?" question tied to your lesson.

4. Have students "translate" vocabulary words into superhero or sports lingo.

In Summary

Humor is central to how boys communicate, bond, and make sense of the world. Whether joking, acting silly, or engaging in playful banter, humor is a tool for coping with stress, connecting with peers, and navigating challenges. Boys often use humor even in serious situations as a way to process emotions and lighten the mood.

Understanding and welcoming boys' natural humor helps create a more engaging and comfortable classroom. When humor is encouraged appropriately, it breaks down tension, fosters trust, and makes learning approachable. While boys' humor often looks different from girls', both styles are valid. Recognizing these differences helps teachers mediate misunderstandings and build empathy between students.

Teasing is a common way boys bond. When it's mutual and lighthearted, it strengthens relationships. Teachers must help boys recognize when teasing crosses the line into bullying, while still allowing space for playful interactions. Likewise, boys need guidance to understand that not everyone shares their style of humor, especially across genders.

Effective humor also depends on timing and context. Boys need to learn when, where, and with whom jokes are appropriate. Teachers model this balance by showing when humor is welcome and gently redirecting it when it's not. This teaches boys social awareness, empathy, and emotional intelligence.

Humor can also build rapport between teachers and students. Being a little playful makes teachers more approachable and encourages creativity, while shared inside jokes and playful traditions can strengthen community and inclusion.

When used wisely, humor becomes a powerful teaching tool. It engages boys, fosters connection, diffuses tension, and creates a classroom where students feel respected, supported, and motivated to learn. By guiding boys to use humor thoughtfully, teachers help them grow not just in behavior, but in social and emotional maturity.

Reflection Questions

1.   How does humor play a role in your classroom culture? Do you think incorporating more playful, lighthearted moments could help foster stronger connections with your students?

2.   Reflect on a time when humor in your classroom either enhanced or disrupted the learning process. What did you learn from that experience?

3.   How can humor be used to help boys process emotions or navigate challenging situations in the classroom?

4.   Do you notice differences in how boys and girls respond to humor in your classroom? How can you make sure humor fosters inclusion rather than division?

5.   What strategies can you use to model appropriate humor for your students? How can you ensure that humor is used as a tool for learning rather than a distraction?

Application Questions

1. Choose a lesson in which you could integrate humor to increase engagement. How can you use playful exaggeration or creative routines to capture the boys' attention?

2. Reflect on the types of humor that resonate best with your boys. Are there any adjustments you can make to your approach to ensure that your humor aligns with their interests and developmental needs?

3. How can you help boys learn to navigate humor in social contexts? Consider teaching them to recognize when their jokes may have crossed a line or become inappropriate.

4. In your classroom, do you currently use humor to reinforce positive behavior or academic success? If not, what small changes could you implement to do so?

5. After using humor more intentionally in your lessons, how will you assess its effectiveness in enhancing student participation and learning? What observations will you make to determine whether your approach to humor is working?

"I believe that those boys who take part in rough, hard play outside of school will not find any need for horseplay in school."

– Theodore Roosevelt

#8 Bring Back Rough Play

Boys Are Physical and Aggressive by Nature

Physical activity and rough play do more than burn energy—they help boys regulate their nervous systems, sharpen focus, and build self-control. When boys engage in sustained physical effort, their bodies calm down and their minds become more receptive to learning.

Have you ever told a boy to stop running or said, "Don't touch him again?" That physical, aggressive energy isn't a flaw—it's how boys are wired. Rather than constantly suppressing it, we can channel it into healthy outlets that improve behavior and deepen learning.

From an early age, boys engage with the world through rough play, physical touch, and physical challenges. They are drawn to action, adventure, and activities that test their strength and endurance. This is their language, and it should be viewed as normal and acceptable.

For decades, boys' physical and aggressive behavior has been viewed in classrooms as out of line or inappropriate. While rough play needs boundaries and boys must be taught there's a time and place for everything, they also need safe spaces to be who they are without being labeled as bad.

If school only lasted a short time and boys had the rest of the day to run hard, get dirty, be active, and roughhouse, this section may not even be necessary. But the reality is that during the school year, boys spend the majority of their waking hours in a classroom. For some, extended daycare adds even more time to that total. This makes it essential to recognize and create space for boys' need to be active and engage in physical rough play during the school day—because for many, school is where they spend a large majority of their young lives.

And if you're thinking that PE or recess takes care of this, the truth is they simply don't provide enough time, intensity, or the right kind of activity to meet boys' needs. A 20-minute recess may allow for a quick game of tag or a few minutes in soccer, but that's a far cry from the sustained, high-energy activity boys naturally crave and need. Left on their own, boys might spend hours inventing games, wrestling, climbing, or competing with each other—activities that push their strength, coordination, and endurance. Compared to that, a short PE game or break in the middle of the day barely scratches the surface.

Physical work like lifting and carrying heavy objects, wrestling, running, and exploring cause and effect, actually helps boys regulate their bodies. It activates large muscle groups and provides deep sensory input, which can calm the nervous system and increase focus afterward. In other words, physical effort and rough play will help boys settle down better than constant reminders to "stop moving."

Channeling Aggression into Strength

Aggression itself is not inherently negative. It's part of a boy's strength—a built-in drive that enables initiative, courage, and resilience. We want boys to grow into men who can stand up for themselves and defend others. But if this natural energy isn't guided properly, it can become destructive—leading to recklessness, unchecked anger, or unhealthy dominance, otherwise known as toxic masculinity. Boys need opportunities to develop discipline over their physical instincts, not suppression of them.

When properly channeled, aggression fuels perseverance, leadership, and protection. Whether it's in sports, defending what's right, or standing up for someone else, boys who learn how to manage their physical strength by being active will carry that strength into adulthood. But if boys aren't allowed to express their physicality while they're young, they won't learn how to harness it in ways that benefit others and society when they are older. They may either suppress it entirely—leading to passivity and weakness—or express it destructively through violence or impulsive anger.

Yes, girls might find roughhousing uncomfortable, just as boys might find deep emotional conversations uncomfortable. We are different—and that's a good thing. We should embrace those differences, not erase them.

A boy who learns self-control through competitive sports or rough play becomes a man who can face challenges with grit. And we need that. A healthy society depends on strong, disciplined men. As G. Michael Hopf famously said in his book *Those Who Remain,* "Weak men create hard times."

What Are We Afraid Of?

Our classrooms should allow for more healthy rough physical engagement—whether it's horseplay, wrestling, or running around and being loud and getting dirty. Boys need to engage their aggressive energy in order to mature and gain control over it. Does that idea make you feel uncomfortable or nervous? You're not alone. Many people immediately picture all the things that could go wrong. Concerns about safety and liability are valid—but they shouldn't override the developmental needs of boys.

Why is it so hard to let boys wrestle, run, or play a little rougher and maybe get a small injury? Some of the hesitation comes from the fear of lawsuits, but much of it comes from how we've been conditioned to think. We've grown overly cautious, viewing every physical interaction as dangerous instead of natural. In the name of safety and order, we've sacrificed something essential about boyhood.

Yes, safety matters. But physical and mental development are just as important. We need to recognize that the risk of injury isn't the enemy—it's part of the process. There must be room within our school systems for boys to engage in rough play—even if it occasionally results in an injury or two.

Boys thrive in environments full of challenge, excitement, and even a little danger. John Eldredge says in his book, "Wild at Heart," boys need "a battle to fight" and "an adventure to live." For many boys, the possibility of injury isn't a deterrent—it's part of the thrill. A scraped knee or bruised elbow is an acceptable part of the process and sometimes seen as a badge of honor. Ever notice that when something is labeled "dangerous," boys become even more intrigued?

With classrooms becoming overly sanitized with safety and boys hearing, "We don't do that here," "You might get hurt," or "That's not safe," they begin to internalize and believe that their natural instincts are wrong. The result? Boys who feel out of place and fall into the fight-or-flight scenario mentioned in the first chapter of this book. As classrooms have adopted a more feminine-centered approach, boys are increasingly pressured to conform to ways of learning and interacting that don't come naturally to them.

Take a look at male-led environments or all-male events. Rough play and physical challenges are expected and essential. They might not always be polite, and there are always some who get hurt, but this builds character and resilience. This is what boys need!

If your nature is more feminine—or you've been trained in the modern education system—these ideas probably feel a bit uncomfortable for you. That's to be expected. Challenging the norms of an established system often is. If you're not sure about this concept, try running these ideas by men outside the education environment— you might be surprised by the perspective they offer.

Let's be honest, our obsession with safety has, ironically, created an unsafe situation for boys. Add in the fear of lawsuits, and we've created an environment that stifles their development.

Of course, we must maintain reasonable safety measures. I would never suggest otherwise. However, fear cannot drive our decisions. Boys need to do "dangerous things carefully," (Jordan Peterson, quoted in Mandy Fabel, Sheridan Press, June 2, 2022)

Understanding that boys are built for movement, competition, and physical interaction is only the first step. The real challenge—and opportunity—comes in creating safe, structured ways for boys to engage their physical energy within the school environment. Instead of trying to suppress or punish their natural drive, we can redirect it into healthy outlets that build discipline, confidence, and connection.

Let's give boys clear boundaries, teach them how to engage in physical play responsibly, and allow them the freedom to be who they are—which could mean an occasional bruise or two.

Practical Strategies for Including Rough Play

The following strategies are designed to help teachers incorporate rough play and physical challenge in age-appropriate and manageable ways. These ideas don't require major curriculum overhauls, just a willingness to rethink how we view movement and play while at school. With clear boundaries, consistent supervision, and the right mindset, you can make room for boys to be boys— without the chaos or risk many might fear.

These aren't just "fun" ideas—they're purposeful practices that speak the language of boys. You'll be giving boys a chance to burn off energy, build strength, and feel at home in your classroom. And when boys feel at home, they're far more likely to learn and thrive.

As always, continue to explore and look for new ways to help boys be more physically active—whether in the classroom, during downtime, or at recess.

A. Arm Wrestling

A great way to release energy and engage in friendly competition is arm wrestling. Be sure to set rules to ensure fairness, such as matching boys of similar size and no overly aggressive behavior. Though sometimes letting a smaller boy challenge a bigger one can be a fun learning experience—as long as the bigger one plays *mostly* fair.

Tips:

1. If it becomes a distraction in class, designate a specific time and place—e.g., during free time or outside.

2. Let students rotate roles if there are more than two. One can be the referee, ensuring everyone stays involved and is playing fair.

B. Physical Responsibility Tasks

Assign tasks that involve lifting, carrying, or rearranging: moving desks and chairs, carrying crates of books, pushing carts, or transporting classroom supplies. These aren't just chores—they're purposeful jobs that tell a boy, "You're strong, trusted, and I need you."

You might be surprised how eagerly boys step up when given responsibility that feels real. Just be very clear about what needs to be done, and avoid micromanaging. Let them solve the physical challenge in their own way. Even simple tasks can become moments of pride when a boy feels like he's wanted and needed.

Tips:

1. Assign rotating physical jobs to give multiple students a chance to lead.

2. Frame the task with purpose ("I need someone strong to carry some things. Who's up for the challenge?").

3. Praise effort and helpfulness to reinforce the value of physical contribution.

4. Assign a "muscle crew" to help reset the room after group activities.

5. For early finishers, offer bonus jobs that involve lifting, organizing, or delivering supplies to other rooms.

C. Obstacle Courses

Boys love a good challenge—especially one that gets them moving and thinking at the same time. You don't need a full gym or any fancy gear to make it happen. With just some desks, masking tape, cones, or outdoor equipment, you can create physical challenges that engage both the body and the brain.

Set up obstacle courses, relay races, timed challenges, or problem-solving tasks that require movement. Crawl under tables, hop over taped lines, carry items across a balance path, or work in teams to build or move something from one place to another. Make it active with purposeful play.

These types of challenges can also be tied to academic content. Spell a word with each completed obstacle. Solve a math problem to unlock the next station. Work together to carry "supplies" across the "lava floor." Be creative!

When boys are physically involved in their learning, their focus sharpens. Their teamwork improves. And perhaps most importantly, they enjoy the process.

Tips:

1. Time the course and let students try to beat their personal best, as well as with each other.

2. Use tape on the floor to create balance lines, zig-zags, or "don't touch" zones.

3. Assign team roles: leader, timer, builder, or navigator.

4. Keep challenges short and goal-oriented (e.g., "beat the clock" or "carry without dropping").

5. Incorporate review questions between physical tasks to reinforce content.

6. Use playground equipment as part of the challenge.

7. Have a quick team debrief afterward to reflect on what went well and what could improve.

D. Pushups, Jumping Jacks, and More

Sometimes boys don't need a full-blown game or competition—they just need to move, but still with purpose. A challenging set of pushups, jumping jacks, squats, or other simple exercises can work wonders. These types of physical activity are easy to manage, require no equipment, and can be done most anywhere. Yet they offer big benefits.

Use them as brain breaks between lessons to help release pent-up energy or for a refocus, like pushups after a quiz. But to make this a real physical challenge, it shouldn't be quick. The goal is to burn off the excess energy boys have—five or ten jumping jacks won't cut it. They need to feel the burn. Otherwise, it's not a challenge. These exercises also build strength, endurance, and—when used consistently—discipline. Plus, it's a great way to start the day and burn off energy.

And yes, these activities can even be used as low-stakes consequences when needed. Instead of lectures or time-outs, a few pushups or squats can offer a physical reset without shaming or discouraging a boy. It's corrective and meets their need for motion while reinforcing boundaries.

 Tips:

1. Use short challenges like "10 pushups before math" or

"20 jumping jacks before lining up."

2. Celebrate improvement—"Last week you did 8, now you're up to 12!"

3. Offer alternatives like wall sits or squats. Have them come up with their own physical challenge.

4. Keep reps short and energetic—aim for 30 seconds or less.

5. Rotate through different exercises to keep it fresh (e.g., mountain climbers, planks, wall sits).

6. Make it fun: do it as a race, play music, or let a student lead.

7. For consequences, keep the tone light but firm: "You're off track—drop and give me twenty."

E. Running and Racing

Simple activities such as sprints, relays, and movement-based races do more than burn off energy—they teach boys how to push themselves, build coordination, and develop teamwork. Boys naturally love to move, and incorporating creative races into the classroom or outdoor activities can channel their energy productively.

Not every race has to be about speed. You can design challenges where the goal is balance, coordination, or problem-solving while moving fast. Add fun twists—like crab walks, bear crawls, or backward sprints—to level the playing field, encourage laughter, and make the activity inclusive.

Tips:

1. Pair boys strategically to mix skill levels and encourage teamwork.

2. Use challenges that reward cooperation (e.g., linked-arm races or team balance walks).

3. Just let them run—there doesn't need to be any reason other than to burn energy and be active.

F. Punching Bags

Punching bags provide a safe outlet for frustration, stress, and pent-up energy. Boys often need ways to physically release tension, and hitting a punching bag can help them regulate their emotions without harming others or their environment.

This doesn't have to be a full-size, gym-quality punching bag. Inflatable or smaller, student-sized bags that bounce back slightly after a hit can work just as well, depending on the age and strength of your students. Punching bags can also be used as part of a discipline strategy—allowing a student to release energy after losing a game or during moments of frustration.

Tips:

1. Set clear boundaries for when and how the bag can be used.

2. Demonstrate proper form to prevent injury.

3. Encourage deep breathing and reflection after the physical release to help boys regain calm and focus.

4. Place a few bags out at recess and see how fast the boys attack them.

G. Playful Wrestling

Boys love to wrestle. They love to test strength and challenge each other physically. Engaging in playful physical contact is natural and instinctive for boys. It may look chaotic, or even dangerous at times, but for boys, this kind of horseplay is one of the ways they bond and blow off steam. It's more than aggression—it's about connection, competition, and confidence.

Providing a structured space for wrestling or playful roughhousing gives boys an outlet for their physical energy in a safe and supervised way. It allows them to engage in something they already want to do—but with boundaries that keep it from getting out of hand. Smacking, grappling, and light shoving may look like fighting to the untrained eye, but in most cases, it's just boys being physical, burning off energy, and doing what they do best, being boys.

This isn't about resolving conflict through fighting. In fact, this type of play often prevents real conflict by giving boys a release valve. It helps them work through frustration physically instead of letting it build into something worse. And it teaches them important lessons: how to read body language, when to back off, and how to handle themselves under pressure.

As boys grow older, this need doesn't go away. Teenage boys still seek out playful physical contact. You will often see them wrestling, shoulder-checking, or roughhousing with friends—as a way to connect and show affection without saying a word. It's developmentally appropriate and emotionally healthy—when done within clear limits.

If indoor spaces and school rules won't allow this kind of play in the classroom, make time for it outside. Though not ideal, a few minutes during recess, gym class, or free time are better than nothing.

 Tips:

1. Establish clear ground rules such as no choking and stopping when someone says "stop."

2. Create a "wrestling zone" with mats or tape boundaries so boys know when and where it's allowed. This is similar to how many classrooms have "Reading Zones."

3. Set rules: no hits to the face, stop when someone taps out, and no jumping on each other.

4. Limit the time and number of participants to keep things manageable.

5. Supervise closely—not to shut it down, but to keep it fair and fun.

6. Praise self-control and mutual respect when you see it during play.

H. Let Them Climb

Boys are drawn to heights. Trees, walls, fences, poles, and playground equipment call to them like magnets. Climbing satisfies a deep developmental need. It builds strength, balance, coordination, and confidence. It also allows boys to test their limits in a way that feels real.

Falling may sound like something to avoid at all costs —but small falls are part of the learning process. Risk is how boys grow and learn. When we remove every challenge or pad every environment, we rob them of the chance to figure things out on their own, learning very real-life lessons. Boys need to learn how to assess danger, navigate awkward movements, and recover from minor setbacks.

That doesn't mean we ignore safety. Quite the opposite. It means we create safe spaces for real challenge. Look for ways to offer supervised, reasonable climbing opportunities. Let them scale rock walls, trees with strong limbs, or monkey bars and slides without constant interruption or calls to, "Be careful." Give them permission to move and climb—let them explore without constant nagging.

If you work in a setting with strict safety rules, think creatively. Building low obstacle courses, balance beams, or allowing them to climb up and over sturdy equipment can help satisfy this drive.

This kind of vertical movement isn't just physical. It's part of their mental development. It gives boys a sense of accomplishment. They went up and conquered something.

Tips:

1. Designate a "climbing zone" during recess or free time.

2. Establish rules: checking branches first, no pushing, climb one at a time, and come down feet first.

3. Incorporate climbing into games, scavenger hunts, or team challenges.

4. Walk the area ahead of time to spot any climbable trees or structures that are safe and sturdy, so you're aware before they try.

5. Start with supervised climbing and gradually give more freedom as trust builds.

I. Foam Swords and Toy Guns

You may have noticed that boys have a knack for turning almost anything into a weapon, such as a sword or a gun. This is normal and should be expected—and allowed —within reasonable limits. Boys love sword fights and playing "war" games. For them, these activities play an important role in development.

To keep things safe and positive, set clear boundaries for this kind of play. For example: no hits above the shoulders or below the waist, everyone must agree to participate, and respect should be emphasized at all times. When guided well, these playful battles provide a healthy outlet for energy and offer valuable opportunities to practice teamwork, creativity, and strategic thinking.

If the idea of weapons used against each other is a concern, help boys channel their energy toward imaginary villains rather than real people. Encourage them to focus on strategy instead of simply attacking. For instance, rather than running around pretending to shoot each other, give them specific goals or obstacles to overcome, against an imaginary enemy.

Please note, I am not suggesting that students should bring toy weapons to school, nor am I advocating for planting the idea of weapon-based play in their minds. This is about recognizing and allowing typical boy behavior— especially among elementary-aged students, and during recess. It refers to those moments when boys pick up sticks or repurpose other items as battle gear in imaginative play.

I'm not suggesting we directly encourage this type of play, but rather that we shouldn't automatically shut it down when it takes place. This kind of imaginative, action-oriented play is a normal part of boys' development, and should be expected and allowed, to some extent.

Tips:

1. Create short matches with time limits.

2. Use it as a themed activity tied to history or literature (e.g., knights, WWII) to reinforce academic content.

3. Encourage the focus to stay on heroic activity and saving the day.

In Summary

I know this topic may feel uncomfortable—especially given the zero-tolerance policies many schools have adopted over the years. Words like "roughhousing" or "play fighting" can raise red flags for educators and parents alike. But we need to recognize that rough physical play is not a threat to learning. In many cases, it's actually a pathway to it.

Boys are wired for movement, action, challenge, and competition. These things aren't distractions from the learning process—they are essential to it. When boys are given appropriate opportunities to move their bodies, test their strength, and engage in active rough play, they come alive. Their energy is channeled in healthy ways, and they engage more fully—emotionally, socially, and academically. You'll often find that a boy who struggles to sit still and focus during a lesson is the same boy who thrives when given space to run, wrestle, or play a physical game. These experiences build more than just muscle—they build confidence, cooperation, and character.

The goal isn't to turn the classroom into a free-for-all play zone. It's to meet boys where they are, respect how they're made, and equip them with the tools they need to grow into capable, confident, and responsible men. That means giving them space to be boys—within clear, respectful boundaries.

Of course, given the potentially controversial nature of this topic, it's important to proceed with wisdom. Always consult with your administrators and communicate clearly with parents before making any major adjustments to normal routines. You don't have to overhaul your entire classroom or school culture overnight. Start small. Consider introducing simple, structured activities like arm wrestling, tug-of-war, or letting boys engage in supervised rough play during recess. Allow space for movement breaks or team-based challenges that involve physical effort. Small steps can make a big difference.

When boys feel seen, understood, and supported in how they naturally play and learn, they don't just behave better—they flourish. And when that happens, everyone wins.

Reflection Questions

1. What was your gut reaction to the idea of allowing rough physical play in the classroom? Why do you think you responded that way?

2. How have you seen boys disciplined for being too physical, even when their intent wasn't harmful? What messages do you think those moments send to the boys involved?

3. Do you believe that aggression can be a positive trait when channeled correctly? Why or why not?

4. How has your own upbringing or personality shaped the way you view risk and roughhousing?

5. What might be lost when we prioritize safety over freedom in how boys are allowed to play?

Application Questions

1. Which of the suggested physical activities (wrestling, pushups, obstacle courses, etc.) could realistically be implemented in your classroom or program?

2. What rules or boundaries would you need to set in order to make rough physical play safe and productive?

3. How can you help boys understand the difference between healthy roughhousing and harmful aggression?

4. What adjustments could you make to your classroom environment to allow for more rough or physical engagement?

5. What conversations would you need to have—with parents, administrators, or colleagues—to begin making space for this kind of play?

Dealing With Behavior Issues

"Too often we forget that discipline really means to teach, not to punish. A disciple is a student, not a recipient of behavioral consequences."

– Daniel J. Siegel

Dealing With Behavior Issues

A Better Way to Handle Behavior

Up to this point, we've explored how to best engage boys—through movement, visuals, competition, humor, and hands-on involvement. These strategies help prevent many behavior issues before they even begin. When boys are active and engaged in ways that match their natural design, discipline problems tend to resolve themselves.

Misbehavior is often due to issues of engagement or misunderstanding, not necessarily bad character. What gets labeled as "bad behavior" is frequently a boy's instinctive response to an environment that doesn't fit him —energy, curiosity, movement, and a need for challenge. Traditional classroom expectations—sitting still, listening quietly, and focusing for long periods of time—often clash with these impulses, making boys seem disruptive.

When this happens, behavior issues aren't rebellion; they are signals. When lessons don't capture a boy's mind or provide an outlet for his physical energy, he creates his own stimulation—tapping a pencil, talking to a friend, drifting off task, or seeking excitement elsewhere. He isn't trying to cause trouble; he's just not interested or is being asked to go against his nature.

This is why understanding and applying the eight strategies for engaging boys is foundational. Lessons rich with movement, competition, creativity, and hands-on exploration can prevent misbehavior better than warnings or consequences ever could. When teachers work with how boys learn instead of against it, behavior improves, focus increases, and boys thrive in a classroom that finally makes sense to them.

Engagement is not just a teaching tool—it's one of the most powerful behavior-management tools available.

Of course, what happens when engagement doesn't eliminate behavior issues? Some challenges stem from deeper factors—lack of self-control, peer conflict, emotional stress, or simple immaturity. Even in a well-structured classroom, speaking the language of boys and using the eight strategies of this book, you can still have trouble. When this happens, how you handle the situation can make all the difference. Here are some things to keep in mind when discipling students:

- Correction needs to have firm boundaries, be structured, and be done respectfully.

- Effective discipline is about growth and maturity, not about control.

- Discipline should teach self-control, clarify expectations, and reinforce the reality of consequences.

- True discipline separates behavior from the individual.

When discipline is rooted in clarity, respect, and a desire to help boys grow, it becomes far more than a reaction to misbehavior. It becomes a tool for shaping character. By providing structure and firm boundaries, teachers create an environment where boys can learn from mistakes, take ownership of their actions, and develop the maturity they need to thrive both inside and outside the classroom.

The Role of Parents in Student Behavior

Parents shape behavior more than any other factor, for better or worse. Many teachers are struggling, not because of what happens in the classroom, but because of what happens at home. Teachers are not parents, nor should they be, yet because children spend most of their day at school, some parenting responsibilities inevitably fall onto educators.

When parents fail to provide structure, consistency, or discipline, teachers often inherit the consequences. This reality can make classroom management harder, but it cannot excuse a lack of standards. The classroom is still the teacher's responsibility, and students must meet classroom expectations regardless of their home environment.

Consider a real-world example from kindergarten: one student arrived at school not yet potty trained. Within the first couple of weeks, the child learned to use the bathroom appropriately at school—not because of parental guidance, but because the teacher held the student to a higher standard. At home, the child still required diapers.

This illustrates a powerful truth: students rise to the expectations set in front of them. Even when home expectations are low, school expectations can be high.

So yes, parents should do their job, but when they don't, it isn't wise to make it harder on yourself by blaming, complaining, and doing nothing. As unfortunate as it is, it's up to you to discipline and hold students to a higher standard. Maintain order and discipline in your classroom. Do what needs to be done, even when others don't.

Three Common Behavior Categories

Misbehavior can show itself in many different ways, but most issues can be grouped into three general categories:

1. **Off-Task Behavior**: Losing focus, becoming disengaged, or struggling to stay involved in the lesson.

2. **Deliberate Defiance**: Purposefully challenging or ignoring rules or authority.

3. **Peer Conflicts**: Arguing, competing for attention, or asserting dominance in unhealthy ways.

The strategies that follow are designed to address each of these three categories, providing practical tools to restore focus, maintain order, and support positive interactions.

We'll begin by exploring strategies for re-engaging off-task students. Every teacher encounters moments when energy, restlessness, or distraction takes over. You will learn clear, actionable steps to redirect behavior, regain focus, and keep lessons moving forward without losing connection or control.

Next, we will address deliberate defiance—those moments when boys purposely cross a line or test boundaries. These situations can escalate quickly if handled emotionally or inconsistently. You will learn how to respond with calm strength, clear expectations, and immediate consequences that correct behavior while preserving dignity.

Finally, we will tackle peer conflicts. Whether in arguments, competition, or misunderstandings, these conflicts can divide or build character—depending on how they are managed. You will discover ways to turn tension into teachable moments that model problem-solving, teamwork, and respect for others.

It's important to note that these strategies are guides, not rigid formulas. Every boy is unique, and no single approach works for every situation. Teachers must consider each student's individual needs, emotional state, and developmental level. Flexibility, careful observation, and thoughtful decision-making are essential to ensure responses are effective, fair, and supportive of both classroom order and student growth.

First Things First: Respect

Before diving into these three behavior categories, we must first explore a foundational principle: respect. Respect is at the heart of how boys respond to correction and discipline. When boys feel respected, even during moments of correction, they are far more likely to listen, reflect, and adjust their behavior. Respect builds trust, and trust opens the door to influence. With this foundation in place, we can examine the three general behavior categories in depth.

Together, these sections form a comprehensive framework for responding to behavior issues with both firmness and respect. This approach helps boys grow in responsibility, self-control, discipline, and emotional maturity, while maintaining a classroom environment that is orderly, engaging, and full of grace.

"I speak to everyone in the same way, whether he is the garbage man or the president of the university." – Albert Einstein

Respect as the Foundation

Respect is Key

At the heart of every effective correction lies one essential ingredient: respect. Without it, even the best strategies fall short. With it, you open the door to authentic change and lasting growth. For boys especially, respect is the language that unlocks cooperation.

Boys carry a deep, often unspoken sense of fairness and honor. De-escalation begins when they feel genuinely respected—even during correction. This doesn't mean lowering standards or avoiding consequences; it means addressing behavior while preserving dignity.

Respect should never be treated as a reward or something to be earned. Much like love, it must be the starting point. Just as we would never withhold love from a child until they've "earned" it, we cannot withhold respect from boys until their behavior improves. For boys, respect functions in much the same way that love does for girls—providing a sense of security, connection, and motivation. While phrases like, "They need to earn my respect," might sound reasonable, in practice they push boys further away and often make matters worse.

When a boy feels respected—even while being corrected—he is far more likely to remain open, reflect, and adjust behavior. Just as someone is more willing to accept correction from someone they know loves and cares for them, boys respond when they feel respected. But when they feel disrespected or humiliated, they often push back, become defensive, or disengage altogether.

For boys, respect and honor are like oxygen. When they feel it, they'll give you their best—and sometimes even more. When they don't, they may disengage or resist entirely. This is why respect matters, whether or not you are addressing behavior issues. Respect should be the guiding principle in every interaction, particularly with boys, just as love should guide all human interactions.

So what does showing respect look like in everyday classroom life?

- Preserving dignity in front of others.
- Acknowledging mistakes without shame.
- Allowing contribution to classroom decisions or problem-solving.
- Trusting students to figure things out on their own, not micromanaging or nagging over every little detail.
- Making eye contact and giving head nods when they are doing well.
- Keeping to your word and following through on promises.
- Pointing out strengths, even on tough days.
- Speaking like you would to an adult.
- Recognizing effort and showing you're proud.
- Listening actively without interrupting.
- Giving choices when possible.
- Demonstrating value and worth, no matter the situation.

When students feel respected in everyday interactions, they'll also feel respected when discipline is required. Trust between teacher and student is key—it creates a safe, predictable environment where correction is viewed not as a personal attack but as guidance meant to help them grow. When respect is the foundation, discipline becomes less about control and more about personal growth—and that's where true maturity begins.

A Personal Lesson in Respect

To understand how deeply respect matters to men—and how easily it can make a difference—let me share a personal story.

I once worked with a private school that, over several years, led me to believe a particular position was being developed for me. I was even asked for input on what the role should include and helped draft a job description. After a year or two of shaping this position that was supposedly meant for me, I was suddenly informed that the school had hired someone else instead.

The head of school brought me into the office, smiling and excited to introduce me to the new hire. She clearly meant well, and didn't make the connection, but in that moment, I felt deeply disrespected—both professionally and personally.

For years, I had given my energy to this school, believing I was part of something we were building together. To be introduced to the person taking the very position I helped create felt dismissive and dishonoring.

Was the person they hired more experienced? Possibly, but whether or not this person was more qualified wasn't the issue—it was how the situation was handled. Respect isn't determined by the outcome, but by the process and care shown along the way. A simple private conversation could have changed everything.

If the head of school had said, "Thank you for all you've done to help shape this position. We value you and hope to work you into a similar role in the future, but at this time it's in our best interest to go with someone else," the experience would have been completely different, for them and for me.

You see, it's not always the event itself—or even how things end—that determines whether something is respectful; it's how it's handled. It wasn't that I didn't get the position (though I was disappointed); it was that it was handled in a way that dismissed me and everything I had poured into the school. Why would I stay after that?

Respect is communicated through tone, timing, and care. For many men, respect is deeply tied to identity and purpose. When handled thoughtfully, even disappointing decisions can strengthen trust and loyalty rather than damage them. It's simply a language that many teachers, and women, miss when working with boys.

Respect Within Discipline

Over the years, I've met teachers who struggle to balance firmness with respect, sometimes confusing respect for being less firm. Respecting students doesn't mean being soft or letting them off the hook, nor does it mean lowering expectations or excusing poor behavior. Like my example above, respecting me wasn't about changing the outcome; it was how it was handled.

True respect works the other way around: it calls out inappropriate actions while holding people accountable, separating the behavior from the person and affirming their potential. It communicates, "I believe in you, and I know you can do better." A simple phrase such as, "I respect you; this doesn't seem like you. Why are you acting this way?" both acknowledges the student's worth and challenges them to rise above the situation.

This kind of respect disarms defensiveness, builds trust, and lays the foundation for real change. Respect becomes the bridge that allows teachers to correct without crushing, and to discipline without damaging.

When paired with structure, respect creates a powerful formula for shaping both behavior and character. Respect reaches the heart; structure shapes the habits. Together, they give boys the security of knowing where the lines are drawn while assuring them that they are valued as individuals.

Rules without respect breed rebellion. Authority without respect breeds resentment. But respect partnered with structure produces responsibility and growth.

Remember this: the key to unlocking any behavior strategy's effectiveness with boys is respect. Without it, everything else becomes noise—words that fall flat, rules that fail to stick, and corrections that only harden resistance. With it, real transformation begins.

Respect Beyond the Individual

A key part of respect is understanding that it goes beyond individuals. Respect isn't just personal—it's relational and environmental. Not only people need to be respected, but places and things.

Since respect is the language of boys, they need to know when that line has been crossed. When boys act disrespectfully, they must be held accountable. This should always be treated as a big deal. Whether it's toward other people or the space they're in, boys need to recognize that disrespect is never acceptable.

Yes, boys have a natural sense of respect—it's built into who they are—but that doesn't mean they are always respectful. Like anyone else, they know how they want to be treated but don't always extend that same courtesy to others. When this happens, don't ignore it or let it slide.

Respect includes recognizing boundaries—lines that shouldn't be crossed—and understanding that crossing them brings predictable consequences. This principle applies not only to personal interactions but also to how boys treat the spaces they occupy. Learning to honor people and places builds personal responsibility and helps them develop awareness of the world around them.

For example, I once had a group of second and third-grade boys acting up in the back of a room during an event. Their behavior was completely inappropriate and disrespectful to both the environment and everyone present. In that moment, they needed to understand the level of respect required. I spoke firmly: "Stop it or get out. You're either participating appropriately, or you need to leave the room. You're disrespecting everyone—and yourselves—by how you're acting." Then I walked away. They quickly corrected their behavior, and there were no further issues. What made the difference? Respect.

Boys respond strongly to the unspoken language of respect. Once they realized their behavior disrespected both the room and themselves, they straightened up. They were naturally motivated by a sense of personal honor, and it mattered to them. Using a firm, confident tone—not a soft or hesitant one—communicated the seriousness of the situation (because respect is serious), and called them to action.

Boys respond best to strength paired with clarity. When clear, consistent boundaries are delivered with respect, boys will normally adjust quickly. In the example above, my firmness gave them exactly what they needed—a clear cue to correct their behavior or get out.

This experience highlights an important principle: while guidance, reflection, and ownership are essential in teaching respect, there are also times when firm, direct intervention is necessary. When boys understand that respect matters—for themselves, for others, and for their environment—they rise to the occasion. You may be surprised by how quickly behavior improves when respect forms the foundation.

The Missing Voice of Respect

The topic of respect provides an important window into the deeper dynamics of today's classroom culture and the broader educational system. When teachers talk about classroom challenges, respect is almost always at the top of the list.

Consider the most common complaints educators express about student behavior: These kids don't respect authority. They don't know how to show respect, and they don't know how to give it. Students ignore directions, push boundaries, challenge authority, and resist correction. These patterns are so widespread that they demand careful attention.

Many factors contribute to this breakdown, a big one being parents, but one of the most overlooked is the absence of strong, healthy masculine leadership within the school environment (really society as a whole).

For boys, respect is not just a classroom expectation. It is a foundational part of how they relate to authority, peers, and the overall environment. Respect shapes how they understand leadership, how they respond to correction, and how they evaluate the adults around them. Because respect is so central to the male experience, the presence or absence of masculinity dramatically influences how respect is understood and practiced in the classroom.

The masculine voice naturally emphasizes respect. It calls students to responsibility, accountability, and clear boundaries. It communicates strength, steadiness, order, and expectations that do not shift with emotion. I am not saying women cannot teach, model, or inspire respect. Many do, and they do it effectively. But the feminine voice is not designed to carry the responsibility of teaching boys respect. That weight naturally belongs to men.

However, this does not exclude women from participating in that process. Female teachers can absolutely teach boys respect, but they do so when it is done through the masculine voice rather than in place of it. In other words, female teachers can reinforce respect, direct respect, and model respect, but the source and framework of respect—the voice boys instinctively respond to—must ultimately come from men. Women can echo it, align with it, and draw strength from it, but they cannot replace its source. Boys learn respect from the masculine presence, not the feminine one.

Both masculine and feminine voices are essential in a child's life. One is not superior to the other. They simply fulfill different roles. Boys need the feminine voice for nurture, connection, and relationship. They need the masculine voice for structure, authority, and respect. When both voices work together, boys thrive.

The challenge is that the modern classroom often functions within one dominant voice. As explored earlier in this book, the educational system has increasingly elevated the feminine voice as the ideal standard for the classroom, while pushing aside the masculine voice as unnecessary. When the masculine voice is diminished or absent, the natural balance between nurture and respect collapses. The result is a school culture where boys consistently struggle with respect.

This is not a criticism of women, nor is it a suggestion that female teachers are incapable of handling issues of respect. Rather, it is a recognition that boys respond differently to different voices. When the masculine influence is removed, a gap is created—one that affects teachers, boys, classrooms, and entire school systems.

When boys are surrounded almost entirely by feminine communication styles, relational cues, and disciplinary approaches, they struggle to understand what respect looks like or why it matters from a masculine perspective, their perspective.

When the masculine voice disappears, so does the message of respect. A major reason so many classrooms struggle with disrespect, apart from home and culture, is that the masculine voice has been muted or removed, and respect is one of the first casualties.

What does this mean? Simply put, in order to restore respect in the classrooms, we must first restore the masculine voice. When masculinity and femininity work together, each fulfilling its proper role, boys learn respect, teachers regain authority, classrooms regain balance, and in return many behavior issues resolve themselves.

In Summary

Respect is the foundation of every effective behavior strategy. It's not a reward or a substitute for discipline—it's the starting point. Respect is the bridge between correction and growth, allowing boys to listen, reflect, and adjust their behavior. When boys feel genuinely respected, they rise to the challenge because their dignity is recognized.

Respect also extends to peers and shared spaces. Boys must learn—often through firm, steady guidance—to respect others and themselves. When they understand that respect is both given and received, it becomes a strong motivator for change. In practice, respect allows correction without shame, high standards without discouragement, and turns misbehavior into opportunities for growth.

This is why strengthening the masculine voice matters. Boys often learn respect through masculine presence, and a classroom that carries a healthy balance of masculine and feminine voices makes respect clearer and more compelling. Structure and nurture work together, creating a culture boys can trust.

In this balanced environment, teachers lead with confidence, expectations are understood, and boys take greater ownership of their behavior. Respect takes root not through harsher discipline, but through steady authority and a classroom culture that honors their potential—helping boys grow into capable, confident young men.

Reflection Questions

1. How do I currently show respect in my classroom during both routine interactions and moments of correction?

2. Can I identify moments when my correction may have unintentionally undermined a student's dignity? What might I do differently next time?

3. How do I balance firmness and reasonableness when addressing misbehavior? Are there areas where I tend to lean too heavily toward one or the other?

4. In what ways do I model respect for peers, the classroom environment, and myself? How might this influence the boys' behavior and attitudes?

5. How do I think boys perceive respect in my classroom? Do they see it as genuine, consistent, and non-negotiable?

Application Questions

1. Identify one specific behavior correction you will approach differently this week to ensure it communicates respect rather than authority alone. What will you say or do?

2. Choose one routine in your classroom (transitions, group work, independent tasks) where you can intentionally reinforce respect. Observe how differently the boys in your class respond.

3. Think of a student who often resists correction. How can you apply respect as a starting point to rebuild trust and encourage better behavior?

4. What is one strategy you can use to teach boys to respect each other and the classroom environment while maintaining your own boundaries?

5. After observing your classroom for a week, what is one concrete change you can make to ensure that respect is consistently paired with structure in all interactions?

"The secret of change is to focus all of your energy not on fighting the old, but on building the new." – Socrates

Dealing With Off-Task Behavior

The Challenge of Technology and Attention

Every teacher today sees the same pattern. Students struggle to focus. They fidget, drift off, interrupt, and lose interest even while watching a short two-minute video. Attention spans that once held steady now flicker in seconds. The reason is no mystery. Modern students are overstimulated. With constant access to screens, fast-paced entertainment, and instant gratification, many children no longer know how to rest their minds or stay with a single task for more than what feels like seconds.

This problem reaches far beyond your classroom. The truth is, you cannot control what happens at home. You cannot limit their screen time after school or change the habits their families allow. Even if both school and home environments were working together, the impact of technology on children's minds would still be a challenge. So while you cannot remove the root problem, you can take responsibility for what happens in your room.

In the face of overstimulation, the most important skill students need is self-discipline. Many children have never practiced sitting quietly, calming their thoughts, or allowing their minds to be still. What previous generations learned naturally through unstructured play and long periods without entertainment, modern students rarely experience. As a result, even simple tasks like sitting quietly for five minutes feel impossible for them.

One practical solution is to intentionally build moments of stillness into your classroom routine. Not an active brain break. Not recess. Not silent work time. Instead, create a brief period each day (maybe multiple times a day) when students are required to do absolutely nothing. Have them sit in their seats, keep their bodies still, and simply be quiet for five to ten minutes.

This practice teaches something many modern children have never learned: how to be bored. How to pause. How to quiet their minds enough to reset their focus.

Another idea is to design projects and use "old school" teaching methods that step away from modern technology. Most classrooms are filled with tools like Promethean boards and Chromebooks—and for good reason. These tools feel familiar to students and often help connect learning for them. But what if you set them aside for a while?

I know of a teacher who did exactly that. He made his classroom tech-free for a month, temporarily replacing the Promethean board with an overhead projector. This is the kind of creative approach teachers can take to help students learn and engage without relying on technology.

While you cannot fix the larger cultural issues of overstimulation and constant screen use, you can create a space where students learn to slow down. By combining moments of stillness, tech-free approaches, and the seven strategies ahead, you will likely start to see improvement. Off-task behavior should decrease as students build the self-control they have been missing.

These approaches are simple but powerful. In a world where children are constantly entertained and moving, one of the most important lessons you can teach them is how to do nothing and not rely on technology. It may feel strange —especially since teachers have worked hard to bring technology into their classrooms and to keep students engaged—but it's exactly what many students need.

With that in mind, let's look at how to manage off-task behavior more generally, apart from the challenges created by technology.

7 Steps for Dealing With Off-Task Behavior

This section introduces seven practical steps for addressing everyday, off-task behavior—the kind that stems from distraction, boredom, or disengagement rather than outright defiance or rebellion. These are the small disruptions that, if left unchecked, can grow into bigger problems, but when handled wisely, become moments to guide boys back on track with minimal effort and conflict.

The first two steps focus on prevention—creating an environment where expectations are clear, routines are strong, and boys feel both supported and challenged to meet those expectations. The remaining five steps outline how to respond when behavior begins to slip—ways to correct, redirect, and refocus without escalating tension, shaming students, or losing control of the classroom climate.

Following each step, you'll find a scenario illustrating how the above strategy could be applied in a classroom setting. The purpose of these scenarios is to demonstrate how the principles are intended to work in theory, as a general concept. Teachers will need to adapt each situation individually, using their judgment to meet the unique needs of the student and the classroom while staying grounded in the core principle.

Each step builds on the last, forming a simple yet powerful framework for classroom correction and redirection. It's designed to preserve respect, protect relationships, and maintain a sense of calm authority. With practice, these steps help turn common off-task misbehavior into opportunities for teaching self-control, responsibility, and growth.

1. Have Clear Expectations

Students thrive in environments that are structured and predictable. Clear expectations help them feel secure and give them freedom within boundaries. When students know what's expected, they're far more likely to stay engaged and behave appropriately.

Explain class rules and expectations simply and age-appropriately—for example, "Raise your hand to speak" or "Listen when someone is talking." Avoid vague or complex language. Fewer, clearer rules keep everyone focused on what matters most.

Be sure to explain why the rules exist. When boys understand the reason—like how being quiet helps everyone learn—they're more likely to cooperate. Boys love knowing the "why" and "how."

Consistency is crucial. Revisit expectations often, especially during transitions, and use gentle reminders like, "Remember to raise your hand." Visual aids—such as posted rules or symbols—help reinforce expectations for visual learners.

Finally, model the behavior you expect. Students learn by watching how you respond and interact. Show respect, patience, and self-control, and they'll follow your example.

Scenario | Establishing Clear Expectations

The school year has just begun, and Ms. Carter is introducing her students to the classroom rules. She gathers them on the carpet and explains the rules to them. One of the rules is raising your hand to speak. "Who can tell me why this is important?" She asks. A student responds, "So everyone gets a turn?" Ms. Carter responds, "Exactly! This way, we can listen and respect each other's comments in turn." She posts the classroom rules on the board and throughout the day, gently reminds students of the rules, and acknowledges when they should be followed.

2. Practice Positive Reinforcement

Instead of focusing solely on correcting misbehavior, shift your energy first towards recognizing the behaviors you want. Praise and attention are powerful motivators—

people often repeat what earns them positive recognition. Teachers do not use this enough!

Use verbal reinforcement to spotlight behavior you want: "Thank you, John, for sitting quietly," or "I appreciate how the front row is ready to listen." This both affirms the students doing well and provides a gentle reminder to others who are not. Often, students will adjust their behavior to receive the same recognition.

Be specific. Vague praise like "Good job" will be less effective than, "Thank you for getting your work to me on time." Specific feedback teaches students exactly what behavior to repeat.

Consistency matters. Praise shouldn't be rare or reserved for exceptional behavior—make it part of your daily routine. The more frequently students are encouraged, the more they internalize that behavior. A classroom that runs on encouragement rather than correction creates a culture where students feel good about themselves, valued, and motivated to succeed.

Scenario | Reinforcing Positive Behavior

As the students work on a group activity, Ms. Carter sees that some students are not focused. She notices James sitting quietly, focused on his work. She says, "Thank you, James, for staying so focused on your work. You are doing a great job!" Soon, other students start following suit. When a few students interrupt, instead of reprimanding them, she continues praising those who are behaving appropriately. "I love how Sarah is waiting patiently for her turn! Thank you, Sarah!" The other students adjust their behavior to gain similar recognition.

3. Utilize Physical Proximity

Physical proximity is a subtle but powerful behavior management tool. Simply moving closer to a distracted and off-task student can often redirect behavior without needing to say a word.

When you notice a child beginning to drift, quietly walking over or standing nearby will gently encourage a refocus. This silent cue preserves the student's dignity and prevents disruptions from escalating unnecessarily.

Instead of calling out misbehavior publicly, proximity offers a non-confrontational intervention. It also allows you to remain engaged with the entire class—answering questions, offering support, and showing students that you're aware and present.

For best results, combine proximity with positive reinforcement: offer a quiet word of encouragement or a nod of approval. This helps build mutual respect and helps keep students on track.

Scenario | Using Proximity to Reinforce Expectations

During independent reading, Ms. Carter notices two students whispering to each other. Without saying a word, she calmly walks over and stands near them. The students immediately notice her presence and refocus on their books. A few minutes later, she uses positive reinforcement and praises their improvement: "I appreciate how you're focusing on your reading. Great job!"

Note for Younger Students and Children with Additional Needs

While the previous steps 1–3 focus on prevention and gentle guidance, younger students—especially preschoolers and those with additional needs—often aren't ready for the steps that follow. These children can't always weigh consequences or redirect themselves yet. So what works instead?

At this age, after applying the above steps 1-3, kids need firm, consistent boundaries. Think of them like a wall that gently stops unwanted behavior. It's not about being harsh—it's about taking away the option to misbehave in a way that's out of their control.

For example, offering a young child the choice between eggs or cupcakes for breakfast sets them up for failure—they will almost always choose what makes them happy in the moment, not what makes sense or what is best long-term. Instead, these children need to be guided and sometimes physically moved into the right action until they begin to learn what is acceptable. In this case, don't give them the option; you choose for them.

Another example is a preschooler who keeps opening a cabinet door. Explaining why it's dangerous or asking them to stop does very little, if anything at all. The most effective response is simply shutting the door every time they open it, securing it so they can't open it again, or removing them from the situation altogether. No discussion, no debate, no asking for their cooperation. Over time, they learn: "This door isn't for me," or forget about it entirely. The physical boundary itself teaches the lesson in a way their minds will process.

Immediate consequences are also important. Young children need to connect negative responses with inappropriate behavior in the moment it occurs. If too much time passes, they won't associate the consequence with the behavior, and the lesson will be lost.

In short, younger students and children with additional needs don't need more explanations or choices—they need consistent, firm boundaries that guide them towards right behavior until they are developmentally able to understand the reasoning behind it. Once they reach that point, they can begin to respond to questions and take ownership of their actions, which is the focus of the following steps.

4. Ask Questions

Before correcting a behavior, ask the student if they know what's going on. Start with a simple question like, "Do you know what you're supposed to be doing right now?" This gives the student a chance to acknowledge responsibility. Then ask, "Why aren't you doing it?" This invites honesty without judgment and can reveal important context—maybe the student is overwhelmed, unsure of the instructions, or distracted by something unrelated, like needing to use the bathroom or cleaning up a knocked-over box of supplies.

Asking questions builds trust and invites reflection. If there is a valid reason for the off-task behavior, help the student find a solution and get them back on task. If there is no valid reason for the misbehavior, have them commit to doing what they are supposed to be doing by asking, "Can you get working again?"

This approach doesn't just resolve the moment; it teaches problem-solving, emotional awareness, and accountability. Asking the simple question, "Do you know what you're supposed to be doing?" should be a go-to habit instead of instantly telling them what to do.

Scenario | Addressing Behavior Through Questions

Ms. Carter notices that Ethan is repeatedly playing with his pencil instead of working on his math assignment. She has already tried positive reinforcement as well as close proximity, but neither of those seems to be working. Instead of immediately correcting him, she asks, "Ethan, what are you supposed to be doing right now?"

He hesitates before answering, "My math sheet..."

She nods, "That's right. Is something making it hard for you to get started?"

Ethan replies, "I don't understand this question." She takes a moment to clarify the instructions, then asks, "Are you able to finish now?" He says yes and begins his work again.

5. Give Them Ownership

Discipline is most effective when students feel a sense of ownership over their behavior. Rather than simply telling a student how to get back on task, involve them in finding the solution.

You've already asked, "What should you be doing right now?"—and in most cases, they already know. Once they identify it, calmly remind them to follow through. Some students will respond right away; others may need a few clear options to choose from. Offering choices gives them a sense of control and increases their investment in the outcome. When they've chosen the right course of action, hold them accountable to doing it. If you have to check back later, remind them that they said it would be done—using their word against them, not yours.

You may need to repeat this process a few times before moving on to step six. Even if it doesn't work perfectly at first, consistency is key. Over time, students learn to develop self-discipline and recognize that they are capable of making better choices and are held responsible for the ones they make.

Scenario | Encouraging Ownership of Behavior

During a small group discussion, two students begin arguing about whose turn it is to speak. Ms. Carter steps in and asks, "What's the problem here?" Both students share their perspectives. She then asks, "How can you fix this problem?" The students think for a moment and decide to take turns by using a talking stick or picking one student to lead the discussion. "Great solution!" she responds, allowing them to take responsibility for their behavior and work through the conflict on their own.

6. Reset With Removal

If a student continues to disrupt despite earlier efforts, it may be necessary to briefly remove them from the group —not as a punishment, but as a chance to reset for private correction.

A short break just outside the room or off to the side can help the student calm down and prepare to return with a better mindset—based on how you interact with them, that is. Use this time to revisit the earlier steps: ask questions, offer support, and help them take responsibility for correcting the situation.

If others are involved, consider addressing the main instigator first, then speak with each one individually to avoid further conflict.

Before reintroducing them to the classroom, clearly restate your expectations and remind them that they have a fresh opportunity to participate appropriately. Let them know exactly how many chances remain before further action will be taken.

It's important to draw a firm line moving forward from here. If the behavior continues, follow through with the consequences you outlined. Don't shift the boundary or offer additional chances. The student needs to understand that their opportunities have been used up at this point— and that consequences are now the next step.

Handled correctly, removal is not a power move but a teaching moment that promotes reflection, responsibility, and readiness to re-engage. It also sends a clear message to other students, because they do not know what was said or done during the removal, and that uncertainty may make them think twice before acting the same way.

Scenario | Temporary Removal to Refocus

David has been repeatedly interrupting class by talking to another student during the lesson despite several reminders and attempts to correct behavior. Ms. Carter asks David to step outside the classroom with her for a moment. Once outside, she says calmly, "David, you're having a hard time focusing and listening while others speak. What's going on?"

David shrugs and stays silent.

"Is something wrong?" she asks. David shakes his head no. "Are you getting bored?" she tries again. David responds with a hesitant "maybe."

Ms. Carter nods and says, "Okay. Take a deep breath and think about what needs to change to stay focussed and listen." Once David offers some ideas, they both agree on a path forward, getting David to agree to the plan.

Then, with a firmer tone, she states, "David, this is your final warning. I know you can follow instructions because you're responsible, and I respect that about you. But if the behavior continues, I'll have to talk with your parents. Do your best—I know you can do it. I'm here to help if you need anything. Can you do this?"

After a short pause, David agrees to return and stays on task for the rest of the lesson.

7. Implement Consequences

If behavior does not improve after following the previous steps, it's time to apply consequences. Whether this involves administrators, parents, or both should follow your organization's procedures. In any case, try to avoid surprising students with actions they weren't expecting (unless the situation is extreme and calls for a stronger response). Boundaries and consequences should be fair and clearly understood before implementation.

Administrators can play a critical role by supporting both the student and the teacher. They help reinforce expectations, provide guidance for next steps, and model consistent procedures. Similarly, parents can offer valuable insight into what might be contributing to a child's behavior—stress at home, sleep issues, emotional challenges, or other factors that aren't visible in the classroom. Understanding these factors allows teachers to respond with more empathy while still maintaining structure and control.

Collaboration is key. Working together ensures that everyone involved—teachers, administrators, and parents —are sending the same message and holding consistent expectations. Discipline is most effective when students see that the adults in their lives are aligned, supportive, and committed to helping them grow. When handled this way, consequences become more than a response, but a teaching moment—an opportunity for students to understand responsibility, reflect on choices, and develop self-control.

Scenario 7 | Implementing Consequences When Needed

Despite previous interventions, Michael continues to disrupt the class and is having trouble complying with the instructions. Ms. Carter decides it's time to involve his parents and a school administrator. She schedules a meeting to discuss his behavior, ensuring that everyone is on the same page with expectations and consequences. The team agrees on a behavior plan, which includes clear steps for improvement and rewards for positive behavior. Over time, Michael gradually improves, understanding that his actions have real consequences but also opportunities for positive change.

In Summary

Every teacher faces behavior challenges, but the difference between frustration and progress often comes down to approach. If you want behavior to change, students must be part of the process. When teachers respond with fairness, respect, and encouragement for personal accountability, discipline becomes more about long-term correction and, at times, connection.

One of the biggest challenges in today's classroom comes from technology and overstimulation. Modern students are constantly exposed to screens, fast-paced entertainment, and instant gratification, making it difficult for them to sit still, focus, or sustain attention even for a moment. While teachers cannot control what students experience at home, they can take charge of their classroom environment. Intentionally building moments of stillness—where students are required to sit quietly and do nothing for five to ten minutes—teaches them how to pause, manage their impulses, and regain focus. Combined with other strategies, this practice helps address off-task behavior caused by overstimulation and lays a foundation for self-discipline.

This chapter has offered a framework for creating classrooms where behavior is addressed through guidance and practical tools that prevent and correct issues in ways that build trust and responsibility. Through clear expectations, positive reinforcement, proximity, and thoughtful questioning, teachers can redirect off-task behavior before it escalates. When correction is needed, ownership, a calm reset, and fair consequences bring accountability without humiliation.

Over time, boys who experience this kind of discipline grow into young men who don't just behave better—they become better.

Reflection Questions

1. When you think of the boys in your classroom, how often do you see behavior issues that stem from boredom rather than intentional disobedience?

2. Which of the seven steps do you naturally lean toward when addressing behavior, and which do you tend to skip or overlook?

3. How comfortable are you with giving students ownership of their behavior rather than controlling every outcome?

4. Have you ever seen discipline handled in a way that preserved a student's dignity? What impact did it have on the classroom atmosphere?

5. How does your current approach to consequences align with the idea that discipline should guide students toward maturity, not just compliance?

Application Questions

1. Write down three clear, simple rules you want to emphasize in your classroom this week. How will you explain the "why" behind each?

2. Think of one student who often struggles with being off-task. Which of the seven steps could you apply differently with them next class?

3. Plan a specific way to use positive reinforcement at least twice during your next lesson. What behavior will you look to affirm?

4. Choose one of the seven steps and create a short, practical script you could use with a student. How might this script help you stay calm, respectful, and consistent in the moment?

5. Outline how you will communicate and enforce consequences consistently, making sure they are both fair and predictable for your students.

"Authority without wisdom is like a heavy axe without an edge–fitter to bruise than polish."

– Anne Bradstreet

Standing Up to Deliberate Defiance

5 Steps for Dealing With Deliberate Defiance

The previous chapter focused on managing off-task behavior—those who struggle with attention, motivation, or basic self-control. But sometimes the issue is much greater. What about the boy who knows the rules and breaks them deliberately? For example, a student is told to sit at their desk. They clearly understand but stand on their chair, maintaining eye contact. This is no accident—it's a test of boundaries.

Boys sometimes challenge authority to see where the limits are, especially when they sense inconsistency or weakness. How you respond in these moments will determine whether your authority strengthens or erodes. The key is to act promptly, firmly, and calmly, with clear, consistent expectations.

Note: Always follow your school's policies and administrative guidance. Procedures for handling deliberate defiance can vary, so consult with your administration to ensure your approach aligns with established directives.

1. Respond Immediately, No Debate

When a student deliberately defies instruction, your first step should be immediate, decisive action. Do not engage in debate or discussion—there's no need to ask why. With deliberate defiance, the reasoning doesn't matter; the behavior itself warrants action. There will be time to discuss the situation later.

Think of it like issuing a ticket as a police officer: your role is to enforce the boundary, not negotiate it. The student knows exactly what they did and that it was wrong. They need to feel your firm, unwavering authority.

Swift action sends two clear messages: instructions matter, and you mean what you say. The longer you spend questioning or explaining, the more control the student gains over the situation. Boys are particularly attuned to power dynamics and notice hesitation. Acting promptly and firmly restores order, reinforces authority, and discourages the behavior from spreading to others.

2. Initiate an Appropriate Consequence

An immediate response should include a consequence that aligns with the infraction and your classroom discipline plan. This could be a short time-out, cleaning up a mess, loss of a privilege, a referral, or contacting a parent —whatever is consistent, reasonable, and proportionate.

Boys learn best through direct cause and effect: "I did this, so this happened." Over-explaining can dilute the message and invite argument. Let the consequence do the explaining for you. The goal is to communicate the lesson clearly, without unnecessary discussion. Consequences reinforce boundaries and show that defiance has predictable, non-negotiable results.

Predictability is key. Students should already know— or at least have an idea—of what happens when they cross a clear line. Have an established plan and follow it consistently. Minor infractions require minor responses; more serious infractions demand appropriately stronger measures. Deliberate defiance is a serious matter and a clear sign of disrespect; it requires an immediate and firm response.

3. Ensure They Understand

While a student is serving the consequence—whether sitting out, completing a task, or losing a privilege—it's important to confirm they fully understand why. In most cases, they already know, but checking comprehension helps reinforce the connection between actions and consequences.

Ask simple, clear questions such as, "Do you understand why you were asked to leave the room?" Give the student a moment to respond. This step isn't about lecturing or rehashing the behavior; it simply confirms that they recognize the cause-and-effect relationship: this action led to this consequence. Once they confirm understanding, leave it there—no additional discussion is necessary.

Ensuring comprehension helps students internalize the lesson and reduces the likelihood of repeated misbehavior. It also communicates fairness and predictability. When boys see that consequences are directly tied to choices, over time they learn accountability and the value of self-regulation.

4. Focus on Positive Engagement

The focus should remain on positive engagement, not shame or guilt. Avoid the old-fashioned "sit and think about what you did" approach. Students already know their behavior was wrong; the goal is for them to experience the ramifications and then move forward.

A good way to do this is by using the downtime between addressing the behavior and the student experiencing the results of their actions to connect briefly on a neutral topic—such as a favorite sport, a project at home, or something they enjoyed in class. Keep this conversation separate from the reason for the discipline. This demonstrates that discipline does not equal rejection. The purpose is to correct behavior, not damage the relationship. When a boy feels valued even during discipline, he learns that authority and respect can coexist.

Do not focus on feelings or "making things right"—this is not a therapy session. There's no need to revisit rules or lecture on expectations. At this point, boys do not need to discuss what happened, explain their emotions, or talk through things. If the consequence is meaningful, it stands on its own. Allow the punishment to teach the lesson, so you don't have to.

What matters more than discussion is reinforcing that the behavior does not diminish your respect for them. Make it clear that it is the behavior that is unacceptable, not the student. It is the behavior that is being punished, not the individual. This approach helps diffuse anger or shame and refocus attention on appropriate classroom behavior far more effectively than any discussion would.

Keeping the focus on the positives—without excusing the bad behavior but keeping it separate—supports the student while making it clear that the behavior is unacceptable. It is possible to have kind, unrelated conversations that support the student while still being firm and enforcing boundaries. Authority that combines firmness with kindness encourages students to change and make better choices.

Boys naturally have the ability to separate situations in their minds. They shouldn't automatically link your relationship with the negative event—unless they are trained to do so. If you simply address the behavior and then continue interacting as normal, boys will generally move on as well and not see you as an enemy, but respect you in your position of authority. Even if they don't immediately, it's okay. What matters is that they understand the behavior is unacceptable, while you continue to show that they themselves are.

5. Move On After Discipline

Once the disciplinary action is complete, transition immediately back to normal classroom routines. Avoid lingering on the incident, rehashing details, or repeating instructions. Handle the situation, move on, and continue teaching.

When the student returns, finishes cleaning up, or completes a time-out, treat them respectfully and give them a clean slate. Avoid subtle reminders such as, "I hope you don't do that again," or "You better have learned your lesson." The matter needs to be closed and already settled.

Obviously, if the student wants to talk about what happened, allow the discussion. But keep the focus on positive behavior and the actions you want to see, rather than dwelling on the negative or what you don't want to see. Again, the punishment, if done appropriately, should be more than enough by itself.

This approach communicates strength, control, and maturity while modeling an important life skill: recovering from poor choices without shame or resentment. Everyone makes mistakes, and we all have moments when it's done intentionally. If you would want a clean record for yourself, extend the same respect to your students.

The goal is a classroom culture where misbehavior leads to predictable consequences, yet respect and restoration follow. Over time, this builds security and trust. Boys respect teachers who are firm but fair—who don't overreact, don't back down, and don't respond out of anger. It's better to be firm and kind than weak and callous.

Handling Repeat Offenders

While these five steps work in most cases, some students will continue to challenge authority no matter how consistent you are. When defiance becomes repeated or escalates, it often points to a deeper issue. This is when collaboration with parents, administrators, and possibly guidance counselors becomes essential. Together, you can identify the root cause and develop a plan for positive change.

In these situations, it's critical to separate the behavior from the student. Maintain firm boundaries and follow through with discipline, but do so from a place of love and respect. For some boys, firm structure and accountability are exactly what they need most.

Finally, remember that your responsibility extends to the whole class. If one student's ongoing defiance disrupts learning or threatens the safety and respect of the group, removal from the classroom may be necessary. While that decision rests with administration, one disruptive student can quickly affect everyone. Boys must learn to respect authority. Disrespect demands immediate action and firm consequences.

In Summary

Deliberate defiance is one of the toughest behaviors teachers face, yet it offers a powerful opportunity to model authority, fairness, and respect. Unlike off-task behavior, defiance is intentional—a choice to test limits or challenge authority. How teachers respond determines whether their authority strengthens or erodes, and whether the student learns accountability or resentment.

This chapter outlined five key steps: respond immediately without debate, apply a consequence, ensure understanding, maintain positive engagement, and move on. Calm, consistent action shows that instructions matter and that defiance brings predictable results. Boys need clear boundaries, firm follow-through, and steady leadership to develop respect for authority and self-control.

Discipline should correct behavior, not attack character. Showing care while holding firm communicates strength and balance, helping boys recover from mistakes without shame. Over time, consistency builds trust and respect in the classroom.

When defiance becomes repeated or escalates, deeper issues may be at play. Collaboration with parents, administrators, or counselors can help identify and address root causes. In such cases, firmness may need to increase, but it must always come from a place of care and respect. Protecting the classroom environment and safety of others remains the top priority. Boys must learn to respect authority. When they don't, it requires immediate action and firm consequences.

Handled wisely, deliberate defiance becomes more than a challenge—it's a teachable moment for resilience, accountability, and growth. Through calm, consistent firmness and care, teachers can turn defiance into development, helping boys learn lessons that last far beyond the classroom.

Reflection Questions

1. How do you currently respond when a student deliberately defies classroom rules? How would you handle the scenario given at the beginning of the chapter about the boy standing on his chair?

2. In what ways could your current approach to defiance maintain or undermine your authority and classroom order?

3. How do you balance firmness with respect when disciplining a student? Can you think of a recent situation where you succeeded or struggled with this balance?

4. Consider the students in your class—who tends to test boundaries most, and why might that be happening?

5. How do you feel about using immediate consequences without lengthy discussion? What challenges might this approach present for you personally or professionally?

Application Questions

1. Identify one recent instance of deliberate defiance in your classroom. How could you apply the five-step framework (respond immediately, consequence, ensure understanding, positive engagement, move on) to handle it differently?

2. What specific consequences could you implement for deliberate defiance that are consistent, fair, and appropriate for your students' developmental levels?

3. How could you proactively communicate boundaries and expectations to reduce the likelihood of defiant behavior?

4. How can you incorporate positive engagement before, during, or after discipline to preserve respect for the student?

5. Plan a personal action step: the next time a student deliberately defies you, how will you respond to maintain authority while reinforcing respect and accountability?

"The quality of our lives depends not on whether or not we have conflicts, but on how we respond to them." – Tom Crum

Coaching Boys Through Conflict With Each Other

Correction Within Conflict

Arguments, flare-ups, and fights—whether in the middle of a competitive game or in the hallway—require attention. This next section explores how to guide boys through conflict with one another, helping them learn to argue without becoming enemies and to walk away stronger, not weaker.

So what do you do when boys start to argue or blame each other for a loss? What do you do when a simple activity turns into a personal attack or argument? Initially, nothing. Resist the urge to jump in immediately. While you should be ready to act as a mediator if or when things get out of hand, it is important to first let them work things out on their own as much as possible.

Boys need opportunities to take ownership of their actions and learn the valuable life lessons that come from resolving conflict constructively. Let them experience some frustration and try working it out themselves first. A bit of tension is normal and should be expected and even allowed; it is part of learning self-control and resilience. However, if conflict escalates into uncontrolled yelling, excessive personal attacks, or physical fighting, it's time to step in.

You do not want things to spiral into a full-on fight, but a few heated words and time to process emotions can be part of learning how to stand one's ground and navigate conflict. Your role is to help them find a healthy balance between letting off steam and moving on productively.

This process may appear a little messy or even counterproductive, especially from a nurturing perspective where conflict is often seen as something to avoid or smooth over quickly. For many boys, venting frustration, pushing back, or even engaging in argumentative conversation is a necessary step before jumping in to fix things. It helps them release pent-up energy and clarify where they stand. If we rush them past this phase or shut it down too soon, we risk bottling up frustration that could surface later in more disruptive or unhealthy ways. Allowing boys space to blow off steam—within respectful limits—helps them process setbacks and prepares them to refocus on solutions rather than aggression.

Letting Off Steam

In general, boys need to let off steam physically. Remember, boys are physical in nature; therefore, they process emotions physically rather than with words. While girls may be more likely to talk or cry through their frustrations, boys carry their stress more physically—through fidgeting, pacing, or sudden bursts of energy, such as punching or throwing.

The key is to redirect that energy into something safe and controlled. Don't fight against their need for movement—you won't win that battle. Instead, work with it. Provide healthy outlets that allow boys to burn off tension before you expect them to sit, focus, or process emotions. Practical examples of this include:

- **Quick Exercises**: pushups, wall sits, or jumping jacks—short, intense bursts that channel energy productively.

- **Active Outburst**: running a lap or two around the playground or track, holding a heavy stack of books, or racing the clock to complete a physical task.

- **Tactile Tools**: stress balls, art clay/slime, punching bag, or something safe to squeeze or smash when frustration peaks.

A few minutes of physical release helps reset a boy's emotional state and clears the mind. Once that steam is released, he's in a far better place to listen, reflect, and talk through the issue.

Trying to reason with a boy who is still charged with pent-up energy usually backfires. But when you give him the chance to be physical first, the conversation that follows is calmer, more productive, and far more likely to lead to lasting change. Much like letting pressure out of a soda bottle before drinking it, boys need the opportunity to let off built-up pressure before dealing with emotions.

These activities are not about punishment for their behavior; it's about letting off steam before the real conflict resolution begins. Without this step, you will just add to the problem and end up losing control of the situation.

I should note that I am not in favor of boys losing their temper and being allowed to throw furniture or disrupt the classroom. When boys cross that line, it must be addressed firmly.

I once worked in a school where a second grader was permitted to push tables and knock over chairs simply because he was upset. The teachers and staff did nothing, as they were not allowed to intervene. This is not the right way to handle boys. Yes, they need ways to let off steam, but they must also learn the difference between releasing frustration and showing disrespect toward people or their environment. That boy should have been directed to let off steam other ways.

Logic Over Emotion

When it's time to sit down and discuss, after cooling down, approach these moments from a logical, practical perspective rather than an emotional or relational one. Instead of trying to force a friendship or insisting they fully process their feelings on the spot, guide the discussion toward the concrete reasons behind the frustration. Acknowledge valid points, but redirect exaggerated or mean-spirited comments. Keep the focus on facts and workable strategies.

Guide them more than instruct them. Ask concrete questions: What happened? What did you expect? Focus the conversation on facts and practical solutions rather than on emotion and their relationship to each other. This is key.

Give them space to discuss what they expected from each other and help them recognize how communication plays a key role in arguing. The goal is to stay grounded in facts and workable strategies, steering them toward solutions rather than letting them get bogged down in emotion, blaming, or personal tension.

One key strength boys bring is their ability to move on quickly once a solution is agreed upon. If both sides can agree on a clear, logical resolution, they will often jump on board without needing to process anything further. For many boys, resolution is based more on logic and outcomes than on feelings and emotions. Recognizing this difference helps you guide boys in a way that works with their natural tendencies, not against them.

Reinforce that arguing is normal but must remain respectful toward the other, even when they think respect is not warranted. When arguing is due to losing in some kind of competition, explain that losing is part of the challenge and that blaming teammates only makes things worse. Yes, winning matters, but working as a team matters more. Teams win together and lose together. Both outcomes are valid and both need to be accepted.

When it comes to general conflicts that are not related to competition, emphasize boundaries and respect. Teach boys to name the behavior or event that upset them rather than attacking the person. For example, "I was upset because you shoved me" is better than "You're a jerk." Teach them to ask for what they need: "Please stop," "Give me space," or "Let's talk after recess." Those simple phrases defuse escalation and model assertive, nonviolent conflict resolution skills.

Deal With Bullying

Not every clash is a teachable, short-term argument. If you notice patterns—one child repeatedly targeting others, covert exclusion, name-calling that follows a student, or physical aggression that reoccurs—treat that as a larger issue. Document incidents, involve administrators, parents, and guardians when it becomes bullying and obvious attacks on others. Firm and quick consequences may be necessary to protect safety and to teach accountability.

Bullying must be taken seriously. For that reason, avoid using the term, "bullying" unless you are sure something more is going on. We must teach this to the students as well. In order for someone to be "bullying" another student, there must be repeated and baseless attacks towards an individual or group.

Unfortunately, the term "bullying" is often used too loosely, which diminishes the seriousness of its true meaning. To preserve the gravity of the word, we should redirect conversations away from labeling behavior as bullying unless it clearly meets the criteria. Using the term carefully ensures that genuine instances of bullying are recognized and addressed appropriately, while preventing misunderstandings or overreactions to normal conflicts or misbehavior.

In Summary

Conflict is inevitable, but it doesn't have to be destructive. When boys are given space to work through disagreements—paired with safe outlets to release tension—they become more capable of reasoning, collaborating, and finding solutions. Not every clash requires adult intervention; in fact, minor disputes can be valuable opportunities for boys to practice self-control, take responsibility, and navigate relationships independently.

However, patterns of aggression, repeated targeting, baseless hatred, or genuine bullying must be addressed promptly, firmly, and with clear consequences to ensure safety and accountability.

Handled thoughtfully, conflict can become more than a problem to solve; it becomes a training ground for resilience, respect, and personal growth. Boys learn that true strength isn't measured by winning fights or asserting dominance, but by taking responsibility for their actions, protecting others, and working together to move forward. These lessons extend far beyond the classroom, preparing them for the challenges of relationships, teamwork, leadership, and problem-solving throughout life.

Physical energy and stress are naturally part of the process. Boys often process emotions through movement rather than words, so providing safe outlets—such as brief exercises, running, or tactile tools—helps them release pent-up energy before they are ready to engage in calm, productive discussion. At the same time, discipline and safety remain essential; physical outbursts that cross boundaries must be addressed promptly to teach limits while maintaining a respectful environment.

Once tension has been released, discussions should emphasize logic, facts, and practical problem-solving rather than emotions. Boys respond best to concrete questions such as: What happened? What did you expect? How can we resolve this? Guiding the conversation in this way promotes respect, teamwork, and accountability, while modeling assertive, nonviolent conflict resolution skills.

Finally, it is crucial to distinguish between normal conflict and bullying. Repeated, targeted attacks—whether physical, verbal, or social—require documentation, intervention, and collaboration with parents and administrators. The term "bullying" should be used carefully to preserve its seriousness, ensuring that genuine cases are recognized and addressed appropriately, while disagreements and arguments remain opportunities for growth and learning.

Reflection Questions

1. Think of a recent disagreement between boys—how might you have allowed more space for them to resolve it before stepping in?

2. How do you typically respond to boys who need to let off steam—do you redirect it or shut it down?

3. Have you ever seen conflict lead to growth and stronger relationships? What made that possible?

4. How comfortable are you with guiding boys toward logical solutions instead of focusing on emotions?

5. What signs help you recognize the difference between normal conflict and bullying that requires firm intervention?

Application Questions

1. Identify one safe and practical outlet you could introduce for boys to release pent-up energy before resolving conflict.

2. Write down two questions you could ask during conflict to redirect the focus toward facts and solutions.

3. Role-play or plan a scenario where two boys begin to argue. Decide how long you will allow them to work it out before stepping in, and outline the specific signs that will tell you it's time to intervene.

4. Choose one simple phrase (e.g., "Please stop," "Let's talk after recess") to teach boys as a tool for respectful conflict resolution.

5. Develop a clear action plan for how you will address repeated targeting or bullying if you see it in your classroom.

"Boys don't need to be fixed. They need to be understood, respected, and given space to become who they were created to be."

– Jeremy Spicer

Closing Thoughts

Your Journey Ahead

Teaching boys is both a privilege and a responsibility. It's a journey filled with moments of insight, laughter, challenge, and growth—both for your students and for you as a teacher. Over the pages of this book, we've explored strategies to help you connect, communicate, and lead boys in ways that honor their unique strengths and masculinity, while fostering respect, curiosity, and resilience.

Remember that these are generalizations; no single strategy works all the time, and no two classrooms are alike. What matters most is your willingness to observe, adapt, and engage with intentionality. Every effort you make to understand your students, to meet them where they are, and to guide them toward their potential matters deeply. These moments may seem small in the day-to-day, but they accumulate into lasting impact—shaping character, sparking confidence, and opening doors to success that last a lifetime.

As you leave this book and step back into your classroom, carry these truths with you:

- **Your Presence Matters**: The way you show up, listen, and respond can be more transformative than any lesson plan or curriculum.

- **Growth is a Process**: Mistakes are opportunities. Struggles are part of learning. Celebrate progress, no matter how incremental.

- **Connection is Key**: Boys respond to respect, firmness, and logic. Combining these with your natural strengths will help you reach them in meaningful ways.

Above all, take encouragement from the fact that you are committed to teaching with purpose. The tools and strategies in this book are not meant to replace who you are—they are meant to expand your influence and effectiveness. You are already a guide, a mentor, and a role model. By applying these strategies thoughtfully, you become an even stronger force for good in the lives of the boys you teach.

Teaching is never easy, but it is always worth it. The energy you pour into understanding and supporting your students does not go unnoticed. It shapes lives, molds character, and leaves a legacy far beyond the walls of your classroom. Keep striving, keep learning, and keep believing in the potential of every boy (and girl) you teach.

You have the tools. You have the knowledge. Most importantly, you have the heart. Now, make a difference— one student, one lesson, one day at a time.

Thank you kindly,
Jeremy Spicer

Recommended Reading

Further Reading and Research

While much of this book comes from my own journey and personal experience, it is also grounded in research that confirms what many of us have seen firsthand. The following list, while not exhaustive, highlights some key works that teachers may find particularly useful. For those who want to explore these ideas further, the following books, reports, and studies provide a rich blend of practical strategies and professional perspectives on understanding and supporting boys in the classroom.

These resources have helped shape the ideas presented in this book and provide insights from experts who have spent years observing, studying, and working with boys and girls in educational settings, even if not every point aligns with my perspective.

By engaging with these works, educators can deepen their understanding, gain new strategies, and connect professional research to their own classroom experience.

Brookings Institution (2021). *The Unreported Gender Gap in High School Graduation Rates*. A report highlighting differences in graduation rates between boys and girls and their implications for educators.

Mandy Fabel (2022). *Doing Dangerous Things Carefully*. The Sheridan Press. A column quoting Jordan Peterson on fostering resilience by allowing children to take risks responsibly.

Walter S. Gilliam et al. (2016). *Do Early Educators' Implicit Biases Regarding Sex and Race Relate to Behavior Expectations and Recommendations of Preschool Expulsions and Suspensions?* Yale University Child Study Center. A study examining how bias can affect early classroom behavior expectations and disciplinary decisions.

Emerson Eggerichs, PhD (2016). *Mother & Son: The Respect Effect.* A practical guide for mothers on building respectful, healthy relationships with sons.

Dan Kindlon & Michael Thompson (2000). *Raising Cain: Protecting the Emotional Life of Boys.* A foundational book exploring boys' emotional and social development and strategies for supporting them.

National Center for Education Statistics (2022). *Undergraduate Enrollment.* A federal report providing data on enrollment trends and gender differences in higher education.

Jay Owens (2016). "Early Childhood Behavior Problems and the Gender Gap in Educational Attainment in the United States." *Sociology of Education,* 89(3). A study linking early behavior challenges to later academic achievement gaps.

Society for the Psychology of Men and Masculinities. American Psychological Association, Division 51. A professional organization producing research and guidance on men's and boys' psychological development.

Christina Hoff Sommers (2000). *The War Against Boys: How Misguided Feminism Is Harming Our Young Men.* A book examining gender disparities in education and how they affect boys.

D. Voyer & S. D. Voyer (2014). "Gender Differences in Scholastic Achievement: A Meta-Analysis." *Psychological Bulletin,* 140(4). A comprehensive analysis of gender differences in academic performance across subjects and levels.

About the Author

Author: Jeremy Spicer

Jeremy brings more than 30 years of experience working with children, along with a deep understanding of how students learn, behave, and grow. His work spans classrooms, ministries, and mentoring environments, giving him a rare blend of practical insight, professional training, and relational wisdom. For over two decades, he has served in the public school system, primarily as a substitute across a wide range of grade levels and school settings. This role has allowed him to observe countless classrooms, teaching styles, and student dynamics, providing him with a broad, firsthand understanding of both the challenges educators face and the strategies that truly work.

A central focus of Jeremy's work has been helping boys succeed, drawing on his deep, intuitive understanding of how they think, speak, and interact with the world. Over time, he has developed and refined practical strategies that enhance focus, promote positive behavior, and create more effective classroom environments. The results are clear and measurable: increased attention, healthier behavior, and stronger learning outcomes for all students.

Jeremy is a Certified School Chaplain through the National School Chaplain Association (NSCA), a role that reflects his commitment to caring for the whole child. His training in pastoral care, combined with his educational background, allows him to support students and educators not only academically, but emotionally and spiritually as well.

His ability to remain calm, present, and practical in high-stress situations is shaped in part by his background in emergency services. Jeremy served as a medic in the

U.S. Army and later worked as an EMT, volunteering within his local community as part of a rescue squad riding the ambulance. These experiences reinforced his commitment to service, teamwork, and caring for others in moments that matter most. He is also a First Aid and CPR Instructor, equipping both adults and young people with essential, life-saving skills.

Jeremy's hands-on approach extends beyond formal education and training. He has extensive experience in handyman work, carpentry, and home repair, and he owns a pool service company where he provides maintenance and support for families in his community. These real-world experiences deepen his understanding of how many boys learn best—through movement, building, problem-solving, and purposeful work. This practical mindset has also shaped his teaching: Jeremy mentors new teachers, leads workshops, and offers hands-on classes that equip students and adults with valuable life skills, from basic home maintenance and carpentry to everyday tasks such as changing a vehicle's oil.

In addition to his work in public schools, Jeremy has served as a children's pastor, camp director, and counselor, mentoring young people in both faith-based and community settings. His training spans child development, psychology, education, and pastoral care, allowing him to approach teaching and mentoring from a well-rounded and thoughtful perspective.

Across every role, Jeremy's passion has remained consistent: supporting the whole child—mind, body, heart, and spirit—while equipping educators and families with tools they can actually use. This book represents the culmination of decades of hands-on experience, careful observation, and a lifelong commitment to helping children thrive and supporting those who serve them.

Glossary of Key Terms

Active Learning: Educational approach where students learn through physical movement, hands-on activities, and direct engagement rather than passive listening. For boys, active learning significantly improves focus, retention, and classroom behavior.

Aggression (Healthy vs. Unhealthy): Natural drive and assertive energy that, when properly channeled, fuels perseverance, courage, and leadership. Unhealthy aggression manifests as uncontrolled anger, violence, or dominance over others. Boys need guidance to transform raw aggressive energy into productive strength.

Bullying: Repeated, baseless, intentional behavior designed to harm or intimidate another person. Distinguished from normal conflict by its pattern of targeting, power imbalance, and persistence. Requires immediate intervention and consequences.

Consequence: Predictable outcome that follows a specific behavior, designed to teach accountability. Natural consequences occur automatically; logical consequences are imposed by authority figures and should be proportionate to the infraction.

Deliberate Defiance: Intentional refusal to follow clear instructions or rules, done with full awareness that the behavior is inappropriate. Requires immediate, firm response to maintain classroom authority and teach respect for boundaries.

Discipline: Process of teaching self-control, responsibility, and appropriate behavior through structure, consequences, and guidance. Effective discipline corrects behavior while preserving dignity and building character. Distinguished from punishment in that its goal is growth, not retribution.

Disengagement: State where a student has mentally or emotionally withdrawn from classroom activities. May appear as daydreaming, apathy, off-task behavior, or resistance. Often signals a mismatch between teaching style and learning needs.

Engagement: Active mental, emotional, and physical participation in learning. Engaged students are focused, interested, and invested in classroom activities. For boys, engagement often requires movement, challenge, and hands-on involvement.

Feminine Language/Voice: Communication style that typically emphasizes relationships, emotional connection, nurture, cooperation, and verbal expression. Naturally gravitates toward creating safe, comfortable, aesthetically pleasing environments. Values harmony, empathy, and social connection as primary teaching tools.

Firmness: Quality of being resolute, consistent, and clear in expectations and consequences. Firmness is not harshness—it communicates strength, reliability, and respect. Boys respond positively to teachers who are firm yet kind.

Generalization: Broad statement that applies to many individuals but not necessarily all. This book uses generalizations about boys and girls as helpful starting points, recognizing individual variations exist.

Goofiness: Playful, silly behavior that creates connection and enjoyment. When appropriately bounded, goofiness helps boys feel comfortable, releases tension, and makes learning more engaging. Needs clear guidelines about timing and context.

Humiliation: Experience of being shamed, embarrassed, or degraded publicly. Destroys trust and damages relationships. Effective discipline avoids humiliation by correcting behavior privately when possible and separating actions from identity.

Humor: Use of wit, playfulness, or comedy to create connection, diffuse tension, or enhance learning. Boys naturally use humor to bond, process emotions, and navigate social situations. Classroom humor should be kind, appropriate, and purposeful.

Leadership: Taking initiative, making decisions, and accepting responsibility for outcomes. Boys develop leadership through opportunities to choose, direct, and experience consequences— both positive and negative.

Logical Consequence: Disciplinary response that directly relates to the misbehavior and teaches a lesson. For example, a student who misuses art supplies loses access to them. More effective than arbitrary punishment.

Masculine Language/Voice: Communication style that typically emphasizes action, directness, logic, physical engagement, and respect. Values strength, structure, challenge, and purpose-driven activity. Uses confident, commanding tone and focuses on problem-solving over emotional processing.

Micromanaging: Excessive control over minor details or constant oversight that prevents students from developing independence. Undermines leadership development and communicates lack of trust or respect.

Off-Task Behavior: Student actions that show distraction, disengagement, or loss of focus—typically not intentional defiance but rather difficulty maintaining attention. May include fidgeting, talking to neighbors, doodling, or daydreaming.

Positive Reinforcement: Acknowledging and praising desired behaviors to increase the likelihood students will repeat those behaviors. More effective than constantly correcting negative behavior. Should be specific rather than generic.

Repeat Offender: Student who consistently engages in the same problematic behavior despite interventions and consequences. May indicate deeper issues requiring collaboration with parents, administrators, or counselors.

Respect: Treating others with dignity, honoring boundaries, and valuing individuals regardless of their behavior or performance. For boys, respect functions as a primary motivator and form of connection—similar to how love functions for girls. Boys will work hard, listen carefully, and behave appropriately for teachers they feel genuinely respect them.

Responsibility: Obligation to complete tasks, fulfill commitments, and accept consequences for one's actions. Boys develop responsibility through leadership opportunities, natural consequences, and being held to high expectations.

Rough Play: Physical, energetic play including wrestling, chasing, playful hitting, or testing strength. When supervised and bounded by clear rules, it helps boys bond, release energy, develop self-control, and learn physical boundaries. Normal and developmentally healthy for boys.

Self-Control: Ability to regulate impulses, manage emotions, and choose appropriate behavior even when it's difficult. Developed gradually through practice, structure, and experiencing consequences. For boys, physical outlets often help build self-control better than verbal reminders.

Self-Discipline: Internal ability to motivate oneself, delay gratification, and maintain focus without external enforcement. Higher-level skill than compliance, as it comes from within rather than from fear of punishment.

Teasing (Playful vs. Hurtful): Playful teasing is mutual, lighthearted banter that strengthens friendships—both boys enjoy it, and roles could reverse. Hurtful teasing is one-sided, causes distress, and crosses into bullying when it's baseless and repeated. Teachers must recognize the difference.

Toxic Masculinity: Unhealthy expression of masculine traits, including aggression used to dominate others, emotional suppression that prevents healthy relationships, and equating masculinity with violence or control. Develops when natural masculine energy isn't properly guided and channeled.